Cannons, Cattle, and Campfires

True Stories about
Settlers, Soldiers, Indians, and Outlaws
on the Pennsylvania Frontier

JOHN L. MOORE

Mechanicsburg, Pennsylvania   USA

Published by Sunbury Press, Inc.
50 West Main Street
Mechanicsburg, Pennsylvania 17055

www.sunburypress.com

Copyright © 2002, 2014 by John L. Moore.
Cover copyright © 2014 by Sunbury Press.

ISBN: 978-1-62006-512-9 (Trade Paperback)
Library of Congress Control Number: 2014956355

FIRST SUNBURY PRESS EDITION: November 2014

Product of the United States of America
0 1 1 2 3 5 8 13 21 34 55

Set in Bookman Old Style
Designed by Lawrence Knorr
Cover by Lawrence Knorr
Cover Art "Escape" by Andrew Knez, Jr.
Edited by Janice Rhayem

Continue the Enlightenment!

JOHN L. MOORE's

FRONTIER PENNSYLVANIA SERIES

Bows, Bullets, & Bears
Cannons, Cattle, & Campfires
Forts, Forests, & Flintlocks
Pioneers, Prisoners, & Peace Pipes
Rivers, Raiders, & Renegades
Settlers, Soldiers, & Scalps
Traders, Travelers, & Tomahawks
Warriors, Wampum, & Wolves

Author's Note on Quotations

I have taken a journalist's approach to writing about the people whose lives and experiences are chronicled in this book. Long dead, they nonetheless speak to us through the many letters, diaries, journals, official reports, depositions, interrogations, examinations, minutes, and memoirs that they left behind.

Whenever possible, I have presented the people I have written about in their own words. My intent is to allow the reader a sense of immediacy with historical figures who lived two or more centuries ago. To accomplish this, I have occasionally omitted phrases or sentences from quotations, and I have employed an ellipsis (...) to indicate where I have done so. In some instances, I have modernized punctuation; and in others, spelling has been modernized.

John L. Moore
Northumberland, PA
October 2014

Dedication

This book is dedicated to the memory of the late Rev. Henry L. Williams of Bethlehem, in appreciation of many years of friendship and encouragement.

Acknowledgments

My thanks to my wife, Jane E. Pritchard-Moore, for editing the manuscript. Thanks also to Robert B. Swift for making many valuable suggestions.

Rum Traders Travel the Tulpehocken Trail

July 1743

Like many Indians living at the forks of the Susquehanna River in the 1740s, Sassoonan had grown up in eastern Pennsylvania. He told white colonists that he was a small boy when William Penn visited Tammany and other Delaware chiefs at Perkasie, in Bucks County in 1683.

As a young man, Sassoonan became chief of the Delawares living in the Schuylkill River Valley. By 1709, as more and more Europeans settled in eastern Pennsylvania, he and many of his followers had moved west to the Susquehanna River and relocated at the mouth of the Paxtang Creek in what is now Harrisburg. He later moved several days' travel up the Susquehanna, and took up residence in the village called Shamokin, located at present-day Sunbury. As a major Delaware leader, or "king," Sassoonan had custody of the tribal records that contained details of important dealings and treaties his band had with the Pennsylvania colonial government as well as with other Indian groups. These records consisted of belts made of wampum, white and blue-black beads fashioned from shells. Wampum was also used as money on the frontier.

In a letter written in July 1747, Conrad Weiser, the Pennsylvania Indian agent, described Sassoonan, whom he called Olumapies, as an aging alcoholic. "Olumapies would have resigned his crown before now, but as he had the keeping of the public treasure consisting of belts of wampum for which he buys liquor, and has been drunk for this two or three years almost constantly. ... It is thought he won't die as long

David Brainerd

as there is a single wampum left in the bag."

Sassoonan wasn't the only Indian at Shamokin who liked to drink. The Rev. David Brainerd, a Presbyterian missionary who visited the town in 1745, reported that he found many drunken Indians there. After he had departed, Moravians from the small colony at Bethlehem along the Lehigh River in eastern

Pennsylvania arrived at Shamokin. They established a permanent mission, which included a gunsmith who repaired rifles and muskets the natives had obtained from white traders.

Shikellamy, an Iroquois sent to the Susquehanna Valley by the Six Nations as a sort of territorial governor over the Indians there, befriended the Moravians, according to the Moravian historian Loskiel. The Iroquois chief "very kindly assisted them in building and defended them against the insults of the drunken Indians," Loskiel wrote. Shikellamy himself never drank, "because, as he expressed it, he never wished to become a fool. He had built his house upon pillars for safety in which he always shut himself up when any drunken frolic was going on in the village."

Loskiel recounted an incident that a missionary had witnessed. A trader in rum came to Shamokin and set up shop in a neighborhood where many Indians were assembled. On the ground he placed "a small barrel into which he had put a straw (and) invited anyone to suck gratis." Many accepted his offer, but one Indian, who approached slowly, suddenly turned and ran off. A while later, he returned, but left again without drinking anything. "But the third time," Loskiel wrote, "he suffered himself to be seduced by the trader to taste a little. He had hardly tasted it before he began to barter all the wampum he had for a dram. After this, he parted with all that he had—even his gun and the blanket he wore—to purchase more."

Much of the liquor at Shamokin was shipped up the Tulpehocken Path. The ancient Indian route is mostly forgotten, but sections of it still course through Pennsylvania's valleys and gaps and over its mountains. Much has been preserved in the form of back country roads, and here and there state highways such as Route 147 and Route 501 follow parts of it.

Sassoonan probably wouldn't recognize the old path. Much of the forest was cleared long ago, the trail

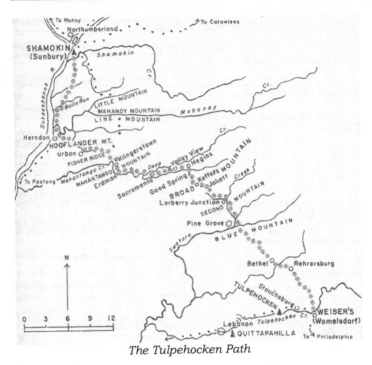

The Tulpehocken Path

itself has been widened and paved over, and many towns have grown up along it. Even so, most of the countryside that it passes remains rural and sparsely populated.

Just as it did during the 1700s, it connects Sunbury in Northumberland County with Womelsdorf, a short distance west of Reading, the county seat of Berks County.

Some 250 years ago, the Tulpehocken Path was a wilderness road that provided one of the few routes that led into the colony's mountainous interior. Native American travelers such as Sassoonan walked it when they went to Philadelphia to see the colonial governor. Traders led long pack trains of horses along it when they hauled merchandise overland to barter with Indian hunters for furs and skins. Missionaries sent into the colony's forested interior by the Moravian

Church at Bethlehem wrote about it in their diaries. War parties from Indian towns along the Susquehanna River followed it when they raided colonial settlements south of the Kittatinny Mountain, and militia soldiers defended the pass where the path led out of the mountains.

Writing in *Indian Paths of Pennsylvania*, the late historian Paul Wallace said that at Shamokin (Sunbury), the trail crossed the Shamokin Creek somewhere in the vicinity of Sunbury's 10th Street Bridge. It climbed the hill just south of the creek, then swung southwest, and headed for the spot where the Mahanoy Mountain stopped at the river's edge. The path followed a ledge around the mountain, which led between a mountainside cliff and the river. It crossed Mahanoy Creek and swung east, taking a gap through the Hooflander Mountain to the present village of Urban. Other modern communities along this path include Klingerstown, Erdman, Sacramento, Valley View, Hegins, Joliet, Ravine, Pine Grove, Bethel, Rehersburg, and Womelsdorf. In colonial times, when it reached Womelsdorf, the Tulpehocken Path tied into east-west trails that led to the sites of the modern cities of Philadelphia, Harrisburg, and, eventually, Pittsburgh. (See *Tulpehocken Trail Traces* by Steve Troutman for details about this section of the path.)

The state has posted historical markers along the route. One marks the place where the trail went through a gap at Klingerstown. Travelers who passed this way included Conrad Weiser and John Bartram on their 1743 journey to visit the Iroquois in western New York

Travelers took this route mainly because they had no other choice. Consider the remarks of Bishop Cammerhof of the Moravian Church. He was traveling from Bethlehem to visit missionaries at Shamokin in January 1748. He had taken a side trail that led through present Dalmatia before joining the Tulpehocken Path near Herndon.

"During the night it froze and the high waters

somewhat subsided," the bishop wrote. "We have before us 20 long miles to Shamokin; also, two bad creeks and the narrowest passes along the river. At 9 o'clock we reached Thomas McKee's, the last white settlement on the river below Shamokin. ... He informed us probably one-half the settlers living along the river died from fever and a cough."

Naturalist John Bartram traveled the Tulpehocken Path during the summer of 1743. The daily journal he kept provides a little of the flavor and color of the trip, which he began on horseback from Philadelphia on July 3.

Here are excerpts:

Atop Blue Mountain, Bartram noted the presence of wild grass as well as an "abundance of fern, oak and chestnut trees."

The trail leading to the valley below took them over terrain that Bartram described as "poor, steep and stony." The travelers ate dinner in a forest of spruce, "then we ascended a great ridge about a mile steep, and terribly stony most of the way," Bartram wrote. "Near the top is a fine though small spring of good water."

As they approached the spring, the travelers suddenly heard "a well-known alarm. ... An enraged rattlesnake ... had put itself into a coiled posture of defense within a dozen yards of our path. ... He had been highly irritated by an Indian dog that barked eagerly at him, but was cunning enough to keep out of his reach." Even so, the travelers killed the snake.

Reaching the site of present Herndon on July 8th: "We crossed the (Mahanoy) creek and rode along a rich bottom near the river for two miles, producing most kinds of our forest trees ..."

Their destination that day was the native town of Shamokin. After crossing the Mahanoy Creek, they rode north over "uneven stony ground producing pitch pine and oak as far as the point of Shamokin Hill whence we had a pleasant prospect of the fall of the river. ...

John Bartram (from the portrait painted by Charles William Peale)

"The stream runs very swift, but canoes or flat-bottom boats may go up or down well enough. The bottom of this descent is washed by Shamokin Creek three rods (48 feet) wide. This we forded to a fruitful bottom half a mile wide, beyond which, two miles (of) good oak land brought us to the town of Shamokin. It contains eight cabins near the river's bank, right opposite the mouth of the West Branch."

Returning from western New York, Bartram's party again passed through Shamokin about five weeks later. The travelers left the Indian town early in the morning of August 15, reached the Mahanoy Creek by midday and continued traveling all afternoon. The trail took them east, through the gap at Klingerstown. They camped for the night somewhere near present-day Valley View.

"This morning I was entertained with the musical howling of a wolf, which I had not heard for many years. ... My companions were too fast asleep to hear it," Bartram wrote in his entry for August 16.

Later that day, the travelers followed the trail as it twisted south, crossing three mountain ridges and going through two valleys forested by spruce. They stopped for dinner at 1:00 p.m.

"We mounted again at 2," Bartram continued. "and climbed up the S. (south) ridge and at the top let our horses rest for they were covered with sweat. We looked for water, but found none. In this search, we found an Indian squaw drying huckleberries. ...

"When we had rested ourselves and our poor tired horses, we led them most of the way for 20 miles. This gave us an opportunity of gathering what quantity we pleased of their berries."

In 1751 a London printer published Bartram's journal as a ninety-four-page book entitled *Observations on the Inhabitants, Climate, Soil, Rivers, Productions, Animals and Other Matters Worthy of Notice Made by Mr. John Bartram in his Travels from Pennsylvania to Onondaga, Oswego and the Lake Ontario in Canada.*

Missionary encounters 'frightful' creature

May 1745

An adventuresome Christian missionary, the Rev. David Brainerd was 27 when he traveled along the Susquehanna River Valley in May 1745 and encountered an Indian with a strong religious bent.

"Of all the sights I ever saw among them, or indeed anywhere else, none appeared so frightful ... as the appearance of one who was a devout and zealous reformer, or rather, restorer, of what he supposed was the ancient religion of the Indians," the Presbyterian clergyman wrote. Working from a mission headquartered in a log house on a hillside along the Delaware River about seven miles north of present-day Easton, the frontier clergyman ministered to Indians living in Pennsylvania and New Jersey during the 1740s. In the course of this work, he made several trips to the Susquehanna Valley and recorded his impressions in a daily journal.

In this dairy, Brainerd rendered a striking sketch of the man, who wore "a coat of bear skins, dressed with the hair on, and hanging down to his toes, a pair of bear-skin stockings, and a great wooden face, painted the one half black, the other tawny, about the color of an Indian's skin, with an extravagant mouth, cut very much awry."

The mask was "fastened to a bearskin cap, which was drawn over his head," Brainerd wrote. In one hand, the Indian held a rattle "that he used for music in his idolatrous worship." The instrument was fashioned from "a dry tortoise-shell, with some corn in it, and the neck of it drawn on to a piece of wood, which made a very convenient handle."

David Brainerd on horseback

Brainerd described in detail what happened next:

As he came forward, he beat his tune with the rattle, and danced with all his might, but did not suffer any part of his body, not so much as his fingers, to be seen. No one would have imagined from his appearance and actions that he could have been a human creature, if they had not had some intimation of it otherwise.

When he came near me, I could not but shrink away from him, although it was then noonday and I knew who it was, his appearance and gestures were so prodigiously frightful. He had a house consecrated to religious uses, with divers (diverse) images cut out upon the several parts of it. I went in and found the ground beat almost as hard as rock with their frequent dancing in it.

I discoursed with him about Christianity, and some of my discourse he seemed to like, but some of it he disliked extremely. He told me that God had taught him his religion, and that he never would turn from it, but wanted to find some that would join heartily with him in it; for the Indians, he said, were grown very degenerate and corrupt. ...

He treated me with uncommon courtesy, and seemed to be hearty in it. ... I was told by the Indians that he opposed their drinking strong liquor with all his power; and that if at any time he could not dissuade them from it by all he could say, he would leave them and go crying into the woods.

"It was manifest that he had a set of religious notions which he had examined into for himself and not taken for granted upon bare tradition. ... While I was discoursing he would sometimes say, 'Now that I like, so God has taught me.' ... Some of his sentiments seemed very just. Yet he utterly denied the existence of a devil," the missionary wrote.

Brainerd concluded that the native preacher "seemed to be sincere, honest, and conscientious in his own way, and according to his own religious notions, which was more than I ever saw in any other pagan."

Even so, the man was "derided among most of the Indians as a precise zealot who made a needless noise about religious matters," the missionary reported.

Preacher Can't Stop 'Heathenish Revel'

August 1745

David Brainerd proved himself as a fire-and-brimstone preacher. Convinced that the Native Americans were followers of Satan, the missionary wasn't a bit shy about telling them that their idolatry was a sure ticket to Hell. His enthusiastic proselytizing appears to have convinced many Indians that his brand of Christianity would lead them to Heaven.

Brainerd spent much of August 1745 spreading his beliefs among Indians at a place in New Jersey he identified as Crossweeksung, southeast of Trenton.

In the preacher's view, some Indians who had been attending his daily sermons were making spiritual progress. His journal entry for Sunday, August 4, for example, noted, "in the evening, when they came to sup together, they would not take a morsel until they had sent to me to come and supplicate (ask) a blessing on their food."

Brainerd regarded this as an important advance, and promptly told them so. "Sundry (many) of them wept, especially when I reminded them how they had in times past eaten their feasts in honor to devils, and neglected to thank God for them."

Two days later, Brainerd's sermonizing about his fear for the souls of the Indians in his audience touched their emotions and produced "many sobs and groans." A few weeks after this, the preacher wrote that he was surprised and pleased when "an old Indian, who had all his days been an idolater, was brought to give up his rattles (which they use for music in their idolatrous feasts and dances) to the other Indians, who quickly destroyed them. This was

BRAINERD PREACHING TO THE INDIANS.

done without any attempt of mine in the affair ... The power of God's word, without any particular application to this sin, ... produced this effect."

From Crossweeksung, the frontier revivalist traveled northwest to a region of Pennsylvania then known as the Forks of the Delaware, a reference to the confluence of the Delaware and Lehigh rivers at present-day Easton.

Brainerd, who used this region as a base for his evangelizing, recruited a Native American as an interpreter. The man's name was Moses Tatamy, a

Delaware Indian of about fifty who had lived in the region for many years.

The Indian, whom Brainerd had hired the summer of 1744, "was well fitted for his work in regard to his acquaintance with the Indian and English language, as well as with the manners of both nations; and in regard to his desire that the Indians should conform to the customs and manners of the English, and especially to their manner of living," Brainerd wrote.

The missionary reported that he had converted the interpreter to Christianity, and by the summer of 1745, the Indian had risen significantly in Brainerd's estimation. Tatamy, he said, "is pretty well acquainted with the pagan notions and customs of his countrymen, and so is the better able now to expose them. He has, I am persuaded, already been, and I trust will yet be, a blessing to the other Indians."

On September 9 the frontier parson and native interpreter set out on a long overland trip to the Susquehanna River. Traveling on horseback, they made good time—120 miles in four days.

By September 13, they reached an Indian town situated at the confluence of the North and West Branches of the Susquehanna River. The town was known as Shamokin, which meant "Place of Eels" in the language of the Delaware Indians, and was "one of the places, and the largest of them, that I visited in May last," Brainerd noted. About 300 people lived in the "upwards of 50 houses," he said.

The travelers were "kindly received and entertained by the Indians, but had little satisfaction by reason of the heathenish dance and revel they then held in the house where I was obliged to lodge, which I could not suppress, though I often entreated them to desist, for the sake of one of their own friends who was then sick in the house, and whose disorder was much aggravated by the noise," the missionary wrote. "Alas! how destitute of natural affection are these poor, uncultivated pagans!"

15

Indians Dance, but Devil Doesn't Show

September 1745

It was fortunate that the Rev. David Brainerd, who had been educated at Yale College in Connecticut, had arranged for an Indian interpreter to accompany him in his missionary work along the Susquehanna River in September 1745. Many of the Indians Brainerd met couldn't speak English, and the fire-and-brimstone preacher didn't know the native languages. Even so, he said he could sense both the power and presence of the Devil among the Indians, whom he found living in spiritual darkness and sacrificing to devils—"led captive by Satan at his will."

At present Sunbury, for example, Brainerd found the Indian town of Shamokin, which he spelled "Shaumoking." He reported that the native community "lies partly on the east side of the river, partly on the west, and partly on a large island in it. ... The Indians of this place are accounted the most drunken, mischievous, and ruffianlike fellows of any in these parts, and Satan seems to have his seat in this town in an eminent manner." This notion was reinforced on September 14 when the clergyman came upon some "miserable, wicked Indians ... (who) were then dancing and reveling as if possessed by the devil."

From Shamokin, he traveled downriver, stopping at an Indian town on a Susquehanna island near the mouth of the Juniata River.

On September 20 he noted in his journal that the Indians there were "very busy in making preparations for a great sacrifice and dance. ... In the evening they met together, nearly a hundred of them, and danced around a large fire, having prepared 10 fat deer for the

16

Indian worship

sacrifice."

They danced all night, sometimes throwing fat into the fire, and this "sometimes raised the flame to a prodigious height, at the same time yelling and shouting in such a manner that they might easily have been heard two miles or more," Brainerd wrote.

September 21 was a Sunday, and the missionary reported that at noon they gathered together all their powwows, (or conjurers,) and set about half a dozen of them to playing their juggling tricks, and acting their frantic distracted postures, in order to find out why they were then so sickly upon the island ...

In this exercise they were engaged for several hours, making all the wild, ridiculous, and distracted motions imaginable; sometimes singing; sometimes howling; sometimes extending their hands to the utmost stretch, spreading all their fingers; and they seemed to push with them, as if they designed to fright something away, or at least keep it off at arm's-end;

sometimes stroking their faces with their hands, then spurting water as fine as mist; sometimes sitting flat on the earth, then bowing down their faces to the ground; wringing their sides, as if in pain and anguish; twisting their faces, turning up their eyes, grunting, puffing, &c."

Brainerd was alarmed.

"Their monstrous actions," he wrote, "... seemed to have something in them, as I thought, peculiarly suited to raise the Devil ... Some of them, I could observe, ... seemed to chant, peep, and mutter with a great degree of warmth and vigor, as if determined to awaken and engage the powers below."

The missionary felt duty-bound to interfere.

I sat at a small distance, not more than 30 feet from them, though undiscovered, with my Bible in my hand, resolving, if possible, to spoil their sport, and prevent their receiving any answers from the infernal world, and there viewed the whole scene. They continued their hideous charms and incantations for more than three hours, until they had all wearied themselves out, although they had in that space of time taken sundry intervals of rest; and at length broke up, I apprehended, without receiving any answer at all.

Ohio Indians Find Sanctuary at Aughwick

September 1754

Deep in the mountains west of the Susquehanna River—beyond the Pennsylvania colony's westernmost settlements, an Indian trader named George Croghan built a trading post on a small hill along Aughwick Creek, south of the Juniata River. From this base, Croghan conducted an extensive trade with the Ohio Indians for a decade. Indians hunted and trapped animals for their furs, then bartered the pelts for the European goods—firearms, manufactured goods of all kinds, clothing, and kegs of liquor—that Croghan and his men had shipped over the Allegheny Mountains on pack trains.

To facilitate his trade, Croghan had established store houses over a wide territory that ranged from Lake Erie on the north to major tributaries of the Ohio River—the Miami and the Scioto—on the south, and he had made many dealings with the Indians living in this region.

In 1747, for instance, during a period of hostility in the Ohio, Croghan had helped the Indians arrange an alliance with the British as well as political friendships with the colonial governors of Pennsylvania and Virginia. The French invasion of the Ohio region in the early 1750s had halted Croghan's trading, and he began to work toward the eventual expulsion of the French Army.

Following Washington's surrender at Fort Necessity in 1754, Croghan met Scaroyady, Tanacharison, and some other pro-British Iroquois Indians as they withdrew from the Ohio country and headed for sanctuary in the seaboard colonies. Croghan invited them to Aughwick Creek, and by late summer, the Iroquois were camped at his post, living as refugees under the auspices of the Pennsylvania governor, James Hamilton.

James Hamilton

Thus, the trader became responsible for the well-being of the Ohio exiles. Governor Hamilton was concerned about the Indians' reputed fondness for alcoholic beverages. "If the Indians be permitted strong liquors, it will be impossible for them to exert their strength or to preserve their understanding," Hamilton said in a letter to Croghan. "I order you to stave every cask wherein any are found, and to return to me the names of the inhabitants as shall presume to bring strong liquors among the Indians."

By early September, some twenty cabins had been constructed at Aughwick to house the Ohio Indians. When word spread along the Ohio that Croghan was putting up the Iroquois at Aughwick Creek, other refugee Indians headed for the trader's post and built huts in the surrounding forest so they could live close by. Soon a sizeable community of Indian refugees was centered around Croghan's station, and events quickly justified the governor's concerns about whiskey at Aughwick. Enterprising frontiersmen such as Louis Montour lost little time in capitalizing upon the Indians' thirst for alcohol. Montour, for instance, knew that they would even swap their trousers and coats to satisfy their cravings for alcohol.

When Conrad Weiser visited Aughwick Creek in early September in his capacity as the Pennsylvania colony's official Indian agent, he found widespread drunkenness.

"Louis Montour ... disturbs them often by bringing strong liquor to them. They cannot help buying and drinking it when it is so near, and Louis sells it very dear to them. ... He sends Indians to the inhabitants to fetch it for him, and Mr. Croghan can by no means prevent it because they keep it in the woods about a mile from his house, and there the Indians will go (after having notice) and drink their clothing and so come back to George Croghan's drunk and naked after."

Weiser added that civilian authorities not only tolerated, but also profited from Montour's venture. "It is a surprising thing that no means can be found to prevent the inhabitants in Cumberland County from selling strong liquor to the Indians. I am credibly informed that some of the magistrates of that county sell the most." The magistrates apparently included a man named Smith, who Weiser said "was at Aughwick, I suppose, to gather some money for liquor he sent."

In September leaders of Delaware and Shawnee bands living in the Ohio country came to Aughwick Creek. Tanacharison had invited them, and he and Weiser attempted to persuade them to side with the British, but the effort failed, and the Shawnee and Delawares returned to their villages where native hunters and trappers now bartered exclusively with

TANACHARISON, OR THE HALF-KING

the French, some of whom operated out of log buildings erected by and taken from traders from Virginia and Pennsylvania.

In October Tanacharison traveled down the Juniata River and then down the Susquehanna to visit his old friend, John Harris, who had established a trading post on the Susquehanna at present-day Harrisburg. The Iroquois leader suddenly took sick and died, and Harris buried him on the river's east shore. Scaroyady, who had shared Tanacharison's work for the past eight years, was appointed to succeed him as the Iroquois half king.

During the winter, another leader of the Ohio Iroquois died at Aughwick. She was Queen Alliquippa, a Seneca who had been head of an Iroquois band on the Ohio. As a young woman, she had met William Penn at New Castle, Delaware. In December 1753 Alliquippa lived in an Indian town near the mouth of the Youghiogheny River. George Washington had visited her there and had written that he gave her two gifts—a coat and "a bottle of rum, which was thought much the best present of the two."

In December conditions on Aughwick Creek prompted George Croghan to write to the Pennsylvania authorities at Philadelphia. Provisions were running low, and the refugee Indians couldn't fend for themselves. "I assure you," Croghan wrote, "all the Indians here have not killed 100 deer this year. They are afraid to go hunting for fear of the enemy."

Croghan explained to the new governor, Robert Morris, that the Indians expected the British to expel the French from the Ohio. "As soon as this government moves, they will unite all their forces and attack the French, but I believe not til then. And they expect the government will supply them here with provisions til spring and clothing for their families til they see what will be done."

The trader wasn't satisfied with Pennsylvania's effort to care for his wards, and he bluntly warned the new governor, "If this government should think proper to support those Indians and do it in a generous manner, I think all the Ohio Indians may be retained in the British interest. But if not done speedily and with spirit, I think it is better (to) give them up without any further expense."

Croghan made it clear that the Indians wanted protection as well as food. "Those people expect a small stockado (stockade) fort made for the necessity of their wives and children as they are afraid of the French Indians coming to attack them," he said.

By late December, Croghan was contemplating the purchase of enough corn and wheat to supply the Indians on Aughwick Creek for the rest of the winter. He hoped the colony would foot the bill. Writing to authorities in Philadelphia, he noted that "the price of grain is rising. ... I am sure provisions will be very dear by spring." He promised, "I shall be as frugal as in my power. The Indians' expenses won't be near as high now as I supply them chiefly with corn. But I think they should have a hog or two sometimes."

Croghan reported that relatives of Indians who had aided the English colonies were experiencing difficulties. "Here is the Half King's family in a poor condition, and Alliquippa, the old queen, is dead, and left several children." Scaroyady was traveling to western New York as a special messenger for Governor Morris "and Scaroyady's wife and seven children should be given something in his absence," Croghan said. To other Indians, experiencing what Croghan regarded as "great want," the trader felt moved to give them "a matchcoat or a shirt ... and to pay messengers that bring news from the Ohio that absolutely should be well paid." He thought it proper that Pennsylvania reimburse him for these expenses.

Croghan complained, too, that frontiersmen continued to bring shipments of liquor to Aughwick Creek, and he asked Governor Morris to prohibit this. At the same time, he explained that he himself intended to provide the Indians with whiskey whenever it suited his purpose. "I am obliged," he explained, "to

23

give them a keg now and then myself for a frolic. ... I do it but once a month. ... I have done it to prevent ill consequences attending the Indians if they should be kept always inflamed with liquors."

The Pennsylvania colony subsidized Croghan's activities throughout the winter of 1754-55, but never erected the log palisade that he wanted built around his post. Nor did any French Indians ever attack the outpost.

Some seventy miles to the southwest, colonial troops from Maryland, Virginia, and South Carolina camped for the winter at a crude defense on a hill overlooking the confluence of the Potomac River and Wills Creek. This was a strategic spot along the Virginia road to the Ohio country, and the colonials had erected a stockade fort to defend it.

By late winter, rumors swept the frontier that King George II of England had sent a large army to America to force the French from the Ohio. Andrew Montour, the Iroquois, and William Harris raised a company of white rangers, then recruited Indians living along the Susquehanna River as well as from Aughwick Creek. They trooped off to the Potomac and joined the colonials at Wills Creek. In early March the governor of Maryland and a British officer recently arrived from England and traveled up the Potomac to inspect the post at Wills Creek. Excitement grew in Pennsylvania, Maryland, and Virginia when the news spread that troop ships from England had sailed into the Potomac and landed in Virginia in mid-March.

Spring 1755 found British troops marching from Alexandria, Virginia, into the mountainous forests of western Maryland and northern Virginia, headed for the post at Wills Creek, now called Fort Cumberland. The commander was General Edward Braddock, an obese Englishman. He was well aware of the presence of the refugee Iroquois at Croghan's post on Aughwick Creek. Indeed, Braddock had even written to Governor Morris about these Indians:

"Acquaint them that I am now on my march with a

Andrew Montour

body of the King's troops to remove the French from their encroachments ... and to restore that (Ohio) country to our allies, the Indians. ... Those Indians must be very well acquainted with that country and may be very useful to me in the source of this expedition. Prevail ... with the able men ... to join me at Wills Creek."

At the same time, Braddock explicitly told the Pennsylvania governor that he didn't want the warriors to bring their families. "They will be very troublesome in camp," General Braddock said. "I doubt not your assembly will take care of the women and children till the return of the men."

The general's attitude created a dilemma from Croghan. For eight months the Pennsylvania Legislature had supported the Aughwick Creek refugees and had since grown weary of the responsibility. The lawmakers had directed "Governor Morris to let me know that they would not maintain them any longer," Croghan wrote.

Croghan, who had also received a copy of Braddock's letter to Morris, advised the governor that the families of many warriors "insist on staying here (at Aughwick) and planting and being supplied by me. ... Yet I must confess I had rather they had all gone (to Fort Cumberland) as I don't expect the Assembly will allow me anything for their maintenance. ... As I shall be chiefly with the army this summer, I wish some orders might be given to provide for those that will be here."

As it turned out, a force of fifty warriors happily set out for Fort Cumberland when the Indians learned that the Englishman wanted their help in fighting the French. With Croghan and a fair number of their women and children accompanying them, the warriors left Aughwick Creek on May 2. Their pace was unhurried, and they followed trails that passed down long valleys and sought out passes in the mountains. On a map, the fort was only seventy miles away, but the route required a one hundred-mile, week-long

A 19th Century artist's impression of the fort during the French and Indian War, as seen from Knobly Mountain.[From Lowdermilk's History of Cumberland.]

journey. They arrived at Fort Cumberland a day or two before General Braddock did.

If pleased to have Indian allies join his expedition, Braddock was also displeased to see that many warriors had brought their families.

Pro-French Indians Murder Missionaries

November 1755

The Moravians, religious enthusiasts from Europe, came to Pennsylvania in the early 1740s. Establishing villages and churches over a wide part of the colony, they soon sent missionaries into the wilderness to minister to the Indians. Their early efforts in Connecticut and New York won converts among the Wampanoags, Mohicans, and some other New England tribes, but conflicts developed with whites who had settled near the missions. By the mid-1740s, the missionaries had brought the Indians in these congregations to the Kittatinny Hills of Northeast Pennsylvania, where they created a large mission, complete with a farm, chapel, and school. They called this mission Gnadenhutten, which meant "tents of grace." Other Moravian missionaries had established themselves at Shamokin, the populous Indian town at the forks of the Susquehanna River, and in the Wyoming Valley on the Susquehanna's North Branch.

In July 1755 a force of Indians and French soldiers defeated an English army that General Edward Braddock had led from Virginia and Maryland across the Allegheny Mountains into western Pennsylvania. The soldiers and the cannons they were lugging were headed towards present-day Pittsburgh, where the French had erected a fort to control the Ohio River Valley and to trade with the Indians. The destruction of the British force encouraged the Indians in the Ohio Country to attack frontier settlements in Pennsylvania, Maryland, and Virginia.

All along the upper Susquehanna River, Delaware Indians had also accepted the hatchet offered by the

French, then used their tomahawks and guns to attack the hamlets and farms of settlers living in the English colonies. In October they killed settlers who had settled along Penns Creek west of the Susquehanna and seized many prisoners.

The war widened rapidly, and the Pennsylvania frontier became a place of great danger for Europeans. Two Moravian missionaries and a blacksmith living at the Indian town of Shamokin (present-day Sunbury), aided by friendly Shawnees, fled the Susquehanna Valley and returned to the Moravian settlements, the largest of which was the fourteen-year-old village of Bethlehem.

In November, Indians from the Susquehanna attacked Gnadenhutten, which the Moravians had established along the Lehigh River at modern Lehighton in Carbon County. Situated north of the Blue Mountain on land the Moravian Church had acquired in 1746, the mission complex included houses, barns, outbuildings and a meeting house. There were approximately sixteen missionaries assigned to Gnadenhutten; at the time, the Indian congregation numbered about seventy men, women, and children.

The mission had been a prosperous one. It was located by the Mahoning Creek, which emptied into the Lehigh at this spot. The stream drained a heavily timbered region. Taking advantage of this abundant natural resource, the missionaries and their converts had constructed a gristmill and sawmill on the Mahoning, a Delaware Indian word that means "at the salt lick." Timber processed at the sawmill went into the building of cabins and quarters for the mission's Indian residents, as well as for the missionaries stationed there. One building, for example, housed unmarried Moravian men assigned to Gnadenhutten. When floods occurred along the Lehigh, the Moravians also shipped lumber processed at the sawmill downstream to Bethlehem, a thriving and growing village of stone and wood structures built on a hill overlooking the Lehigh River.

Gnadenhutten stood at a strategic spot along an Indian trail long used by travelers going from the Susquehanna's North Branch to the Forks of the Delaware. The Moravians and their Indian converts had used the southern section of this trail, known as the Lehigh Path, in traveling the twenty-five miles between Gnadenhutten and Bethlehem, which the Moravians had founded in 1741. With the outbreak of war, this path had become a popular route not only for war parties, but also for armed patrols of colonial rangers and other troops from the European settlements.

A Moravian bishop, J. Mortimer Levering, drew upon manuscript sources in the Moravian Church archives at Bethlehem in describing the Gnadenhutten massacre. He reported that the evening of November 24, the missionaries had gathered in the main house for the evening meal. There were fifteen adults and a fourteen-month-old child. Suddenly, the dogs started to bark, and the missionaries heard people coming up to the mission complex. A ranger company had passed by earlier that day, and the Moravians had expected the soldiers to return to the mission and to spend the night. But these visitors were hostile Indians—not colonial troops. They had come down from the Susquehanna River Valley to the north. They entered the complex, rushed the house, and opened fire. Several of the Moravians died instantly, but others managed to flee to the garret, where they locked themselves in. Unable to open the trap door, the warriors torched the house.

As the building burned, three missionaries managed to jump from the garret window, but four others perished in the fire. One of those who jumped was Susanna Partsch. She fled into the woods and hid behind a tree. Temporarily safe in the forest, she watched the attack play out. She counted a dozen warriors and watched them loot the store, spring house, and kitchen. Then they went from building to building and torched the place, beginning with the barn and proceeding to the kitchen and bakery, the residence of the unmarried men, and, finally, the main building, which housed the chapel. As the mission burned, the Indians had a feast by firelight. Toward midnight, they took as much loot as they could carry and left, walking toward the trail that led to the Wyoming Valley.

When she was certain that the warriors were gone, Susanna Partsch cautiously walked down the Mahoning to the Lehigh River. She found a hollow tree, got inside, and stayed hidden until morning.

Another missionary who jumped from the window was less fortunate. George Christian Fabricus, a native of Denmark who was nearly forty, had followed Partsch out of the structure, but the warriors pursued him and foiled his attempt to flee. According to Bishop Levering, when a party of rescuers reached the mission the next morning, "… in the square, they came upon the body of Fabricus, pierced with bullets, scalped and mutilated, and watched over by … his dog." These rangers also found that the war party had left a calling card of sorts—a blanket and a hat left on a tree stump and pierced by a knife.

Fabricus, the mission's chaplain, had learned the language of the Delaware Indians and taught the Indian children who lived at the mission.

Although the Indians had burned the mission on the Lehigh River's west shore, the warriors hadn't disturbed the approximately twenty dwellings where the Indians lived on the flats on the river's east bank. This was little consolation to the Christian Indians. As the attack took place across the river, they fled into the forest. About thirty of these Indians gathered in the woods along the trail leading to Bethlehem. Joachim Sensemann, a missionary who had survived the massacre, came upon them the next day as he made his way to Bethlehem. He took them along, and this band of fugitives reached the Moravian settlement in the afternoon. In time, all seventy of the mission

Indians arrived safely in Bethlehem, where the church accommodated them in special quarters that Bishop Levering described as "the Indian House."

By midday November 25, the mission at Gnadenhutten was abandoned. The only person who remained was the missionary Shebosh. Concerned that some Indians from the mission congregation might be hiding in the nearby woods, he stayed on for a while. He wanted to be present—and be seen—in case any Indians belonging to the congregation returned to the town.

Many of the missionaries were husband-and-wife teams. Martin and Susanna Nitschmann were such a couple. They had been assigned to Gnadenhutten for less than four months. Martin died in the initial shooting; though wounded by a gunshot, Susanna survived the attack only to be carried off as a prisoner by the leader of the war party. In captivity, she lived for a while on the Susquehanna River's North Branch at Wyoming. Baptized Indians whom the Moravian Church accepted as responsible and credible sources reported that her captor eventually took her farther up the North Branch and that, deeply depressed, she died at Tioga, apparently some time prior to July 1756.

The night of the massacre, the flames were so bright that at Bethlehem, "the light of the burning buildings, although nearly 30 miles distant and with the ridge of the Blue Mountain between, was clearly seen," reported Moravian chronicler John Heckewelder in *Narrative of the Mission of the United Brethren Among the Delaware and Mohegan Indians*.

After this, pioneer families in northeastern Pennsylvania fled their frontier homesteads in a panic. They headed for more settled areas south of the Blue Mountain and farther away from the mountain trails that war parties were likely to use. In turn, many of the peaceful Indians who lived at Gnadenhutten fled into the woods. They feared the hostile warriors as well as parties of armed whites who were bent on killing Indians as much as protecting the European settlements.

The Moravians erected stockades around the villages of Bethlehem and Nazareth, and soon the fortified towns attracted large numbers of refugees—Indians as well as whites. The Moravians accepted these fugitives. As Charles T. Ledderhose wrote in his 1855 biography of the Bethlehem bishop, Augustus Gottlieb Spangenberg, "The Indian congregation at Gnadenhutten had been scattered ... but the greater part of these scattered sheep by degrees found their way to Bethlehem, which now became a place of refuge for many other persons. About 600 men and women had to be cared for and protected during the severe winter."

The terror that many of these refugees felt was heart wrenching. The bishop's biography recounts an instance: "One day a man on his flight from the Indians beyond the mountains came to Bethlehem and cried, 'I will not go another step. If I am not safe among the children of God, where shall I be safe?'" The Moravians promptly gave the man refuge.

The Pennsylvania Colony was not wholly unprepared for attacks such as these. Indeed, Braddock's defeat in July had prompted many frontier settlers to organize patrols. For example, in the valley of the Saucon Creek, which empties into the Lehigh River a few miles south and east of Bethlehem, the men organized a company of rangers in August. A prominent settler, a German emigrant named Christian Laubach, became its captain. A blacksmith who had erected a combination grist-and-saw mill along a stream in the Saucon Valley, Laubach had been a soldier in Europe. Although he was in his mid-fifties, Captain Laubach mobilized the Saucon Rangers after the Gnadenhutten massacre. On November 26, two nights after the attack, Laubach and his troops were in Nazareth, about seven miles north of Bethlehem. They spent the night at the Rose Inn. The next day, the ranger company patrolled the woods around Nazareth, where many farm families had headed for refuge. When word arrived that an Indian war party had been spotted in a nearby gap in the mountains, the rangers headed north to find them.

Ben Franklin Leads Militia into Bethlehem

December 1755

In December Benjamin Franklin rode into Bethlehem at the head of a column of Pennsylvania soldiers. He had been sent by the government at Philadelphia, and his mission was to organize a formal defense of the region. If he had a military rank, he didn't flaunt it. The colonial legislature had appointed him head of its Committee of Defense, and it may be that this was Franklin's only official title at this point. But the forty-nine-year-old colonial clearly had assumed command. When he arrived in Bethlehem with a mounted escort, the Moravians recognized the Philadelphian as "general lieutenant and commander-in-chief of our county."

As winter set in, Franklin set about organizing a force for protecting the colony's northern frontier and erecting log forts along the Blue Mountain. In general, Franklin entertained a low opinion of these crude defenses, which he derided as "miserable" and even "contemptible," but said he believed they would generally provide "a sufficient defense against Indians who have no cannon."

As he entered Bethlehem, Franklin was surprised to see the peaceable Moravians had fortified their community.

"The principal buildings were defended by a stockade," Franklin wrote in *The Autobiography of Benjamin Franklin*.

"They had purchased a quantity of arms and ammunition from New York, and had even placed quantities of small paving stones between the windows of their high stone houses, for their women to throw

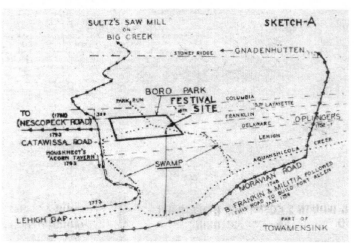

This map shows roughly the 1748 Moravian Road to Gnadenhutten and the path followed by Benjamin Franklin.

down upon the heads of any Indians that should attempt to force into them," Franklin reported.

Pennsylvania authorities ordered a company of soldiers to march to the ruins of Gnadenhutten in early December. Commanded by Captain William Hays, these soldiers appear to have set up an outpost among some buildings that had survived the attack in November. The colonials established themselves at the site of present-day Weissport, along the Indian trail that linked the Lehigh River at Bethlehem with Nescopeck on the North Branch.

Although the war party had torched some buildings at Gnadenhutten, they had spared the cabins where the Indians lived as well as the mills and a church, or chapel, that the congregation had built. The mills were loaded with grain harvested from the mission farm.

At first, Hays and his men were vigilant in guarding the mills and the cabins, but when several days passed without any sign of hostiles, they relaxed. By December 31, the Lehigh River had frozen over. New Year's Day must have been pleasant, because

Hays let his soldiers go ice-skating across from the fort.

The men were enjoying themselves when "at some distance higher up, where the river made a bend, they espied two Indians, apparently amusing themselves in the same manner" reported Heckewelder, the Moravian chronicler. The Indians ran upriver on the ice, with the soldiers in pursuit. Suddenly, "a party that lay in ambush ... rushed forth from their hiding place and put them (the soldiers) to death," Heckewelder said.

Downstream, the surviving militiamen decided there were too many Indians to fight back, so they abandoned the post and retreated to Bethlehem.

"The savages," Heckewelder wrote, "after seizing ... as much property as they could carry off, set fire to the fort, to the houses of the Indians, and to the ... mills."

Franklin's Force Erects Four Stockade Forts

January 1756

We think of Benjamin Franklin primarily as a printer, politician, and signer of the Declaration of Independence, but as a military leader, the Philadelphian was also a builder of forts along the Pennsylvania frontier.

In 1755 and 1756 Franklin was a loyal Englishman, and his foes included Indian warriors from the Susquehanna River Valley who had taken up the hatchet on behalf of France, England's enemy throughout the French and Indian War.

In attacking the Pennsylvania settlements, these Indians used trickery, tomahawks, and bows and arrows quite skillfully. They frequently got the better of the colonial troops and frontiersmen armed with superior weapons. One example: their successful

Benjamin Franklin

strategy in defeating the soldiers who had been ice-skating on the Lehigh.

The incident prompted Franklin to take personal command of the soldiers assigned to rebuild the post. He also intended to build a second fort in the Minisinks section of the Upper Delaware River Valley as well as forts at two other locations. He assembled his soldiers at Bethlehem and prepared to march off into the Kittatinny Mountains, some thirty miles north of the Moravian town, in January. Franklin's small staff included his only son, William. "My son, who had … been an officer in the army raised against Canada, was my aide-de-camp and of great use to me," he wrote.

"Just before we left Bethlehem, 11 farmers, who had been driven from their plantations by the Indians, came to me requesting a supply of firearms, that they might go back and fetch off their cattle," Franklin wrote in his autobiography.

The commander quickly granted the request, and "I gave them each a gun with suitable ammunition." Traveling on horseback, the farmers rapidly rode north toward their settlements along the foot of the Blue Mountain, but Franklin's column, using five wagons the Moravians gave them to transport "our tools, stores, baggage, etc.," moved much more slowly.

"We had not marched many miles before it began to rain, and it continued raining all day; there were no habitations on the road to shelter us till we arrived near night at the house of a German, where, and in his barn, we were all huddled together, as wet as water could make us," Franklin reported.

As Franklin remarked, "It was well we were not attacked in our march, for our arms were of the most ordinary sort, and our men could not keep their gun locks dry."

Franklin soon learned that the farmers had not only encountered heavy rains, but also something Franklin's force had not—a war party.

When the Indians attacked, the farmers tried to

defend themselves with the rifles they had received from Franklin, but the "guns would not go off, the priming being wet with the rain." Without firearms, they couldn't defend themselves, and the tomahawk-wielding warriors soon killed ten of the eleven men.

By morning, the weather had cleared, and Franklin's column continued its two-day march to Gnadenhutten. The militiamen began their occupation of the place by burying the bodies of Captain Hays's men. They "had been half interred by the country people," Franklin wrote.

For temporary shelter, the soldiers took lumber from piles of boards at the saw mill and used it to construct crude huts. This task had a high priority "as we had no tents," Franklin said.

Franklin goes on:

The next morning, our fort was planned and marked out, the circumference measuring four hundred and fifty-five feet, which would require as many palisades to be made of trees, one with another, of a foot diameter each. Our axes, of which we had seventy, were immediately set to work to cut down trees, and, our men being dexterous in the use of them, great dispatch was made.

Seeing the trees fall so fast, I had the curiosity to look at my watch when two men began to cut at a pine; in six minutes they had it upon the ground, and I found it of fourteen inches diameter. Each pine made three palisades of eighteen feet long, pointed at one end.

While these were preparing, our other men dug a trench all round, of three feet deep, in which the palisades were to be planted; and our wagons, the bodies being taken off, and the fore and hind wheels separated by taking out the pin which united the two parts of the perch, we had ten carriages, with two horses each, to bring the palisades from the woods to the spot.

When they were set up, our carpenters built a stage of boards all round within, about six feet high, for the men to stand on when to fire through the loopholes. We had one swivel gun, which we mounted on one of the angles, and fired it as soon as fixed, to let the Indians know, if any were within hearing, that we had such pieces; and thus our fort, if such a magnificent name may be given to so miserable a stockade, was finished in a week, though it rained so hard every other day that the men could not work.

Franklin used the occasion for observing some contrasts in human nature:

When men are employed, they are best contented; for on the days they worked they were good-natured and cheerful, and, with the consciousness of having done a good day's work, they spent the evening jollily; but on our idle days they were mutinous and quarrelsome, finding fault with their pork, the bread, etc., and in continual ill-humor, which put me in mind of a sea-captain, whose rule it was to keep his men constantly at work; and, when his mate once told him that they had done everything, and there was nothing further to employ them about, 'Oh,' says he, 'Make them scour the anchor."

At week's end, with the stockade erected and outfitted with guns, the commander decided the time had come to send out scouts and determine whether any hostile warriors were lurking about. "Finding ourselves now posted securely, and having a place to retreat to on occasion, we ventured out in parties to scour the adjacent country," he wrote.

We met with no Indians, but we found the places on the neighboring hills where they had lain to watch our proceedings. There was an art in their contrivance of those places that seems worth mention. It being winter, a fire was necessary for them; but a common fire on the surface of the ground would by its light have discovered their position at a distance.

They had therefore dug holes in the ground about three feet diameter, and somewhat deeper; we saw where they had with their hatchets cut off the charcoal from the sides of burnt logs lying in the woods. With these coals they had made small fires in the bottom of the holes, and we observed among the weeds and grass the prints of their bodies, made by their laying all round, with their legs hanging down in the holes to keep their feet warm, which, with them, is an essential point. This kind of fire, so managed, could not discover them, either by its light, flame, sparks, or even smoke. It appeared that their number was not great, and it seems they saw we were too many to be attacked by them with prospect of advantage.

Chaplain's Rum Draws Troops to Services

January 1756

Among the men who took part in the Gnadenhutten campaign was Charles Beatty, a frontier preacher whom Benjamin Franklin described as "a zealous Presbyterian." Beatty, who had signed on as the expedition's chaplain, held daily worship

Rev. Charles Beatty

services, but Franklin wrote that he soon "complained to me that the men did not generally attend his prayers and exhortations."

Ever the realist, Franklin pointed out to the chaplain that the rank-and-file troops were prompt to report for their daily rations of liquor.

"When they enlisted, they were promised, besides pay and provisions, a gill of rum a day, which was punctually served out to them, half in the morning, and the other half in the evening; and I observed they were as punctual in attending to receive it," Franklin wrote.

"... I said to Mr. Beatty, 'It is, perhaps, below the dignity of your profession to act as steward of the rum, but if you were to deal it out only just after prayers, you would have them all about you.'"

Franklin reported Beatty did as he had suggested, and, "with the help of a few hands to measure out the liquor, ... never were prayers more generally and more punctually attended; so that I thought this method preferable to the punishment inflicted by some military laws for non-attendance on divine service."

In addition to building Fort Allen at Gnadenhutten, Franklin had responsibility for building three new forts in eastern Pennsylvania. To do this, he sent men and supplies into the southern Pocono Mountains with orders to complete Fort Hamilton at present-day Stroudsburg in Monroe County. He assigned other troops to erect a post called Fort Norris near present Kresgeville, also in Monroe County. Still, other troops he sent to "the forks of the Schuylkill" in what is now Schuylkill County, and they built a stockade post that was eventually called Fort Franklin.

If colorful, Franklin's stint as a field commander was a brief one. "I had hardly ... got my fort well stored with provisions, when I received a letter from the governor, acquainting me that he had called the Assembly, and wished my attendance there, if the posture of affairs on the frontiers was such that my remaining there was no longer necessary," Franklin wrote.

My ... forts being now completed, and the inhabitants contented to remain on their farms under that protection, I resolved to return; the more willingly, as a New England officer, Colonel Clapham, experienced in Indian war, being on a visit to our establishment, consented to accept the command.

I gave him a commission, and, parading the garrison, had it read before them, and introduced him to them as an officer who, from his skill in military affairs was much more fit to command them than myself; and, giving them a little exhortation, took my leave. I was escorted as far as Bethlehem, where I rested a few days to recover from the fatigue I had undergone. The first night, being in a good bed, I could hardly sleep, it was so different from my hard lodging on the floor of our hut at Gnadenhutten wrapped only in a blanket or two.

Frontier Farmers Often Lack Guns, Powder

Autumn 1755

The frontiersmen of colonial Pennsylvania tended to be farmers rather than soldiers. Many didn't feel a need to own firearms and, except for a few who had been in the military, hadn't ever learned how to shoot.

This was largely because the peace that William Penn established in 1681 with the Native Americans of eastern Pennsylvania lasted nearly seventy-five years. Although most other European colonies fought numerous Indian wars during this time, the Quaker colony enjoyed a prolonged period of war-free prosperity.

Most Pennsylvania colonists preferred the fields to the forests and worked hard to chop down the old-growth forests that sprawled across the rolling countryside and up and down the colony's many valleys. They even killed the grandest and tallest of trees that stood on land they wanted to plant rye, oats, flax, and wheat on. They used some of the oak and pine logs to make cabins and outbuildings and kept enough lumber to make tables, benches, and frames for their beds. They burned the rest either as fuel for their cooking fires or to keep their families warm in the winter. Sometimes settlers who lived along rivers and large streams used logs to make dugout canoes, as the Indians did.

These hardy settlers could swing an ax, plow a field, and raise a barn with considerable skill. As long as the frontier remained peaceful, these abilities sufficed. But when the French and Indian War erupted during the autumn of 1755, these farmers often lacked the experience and training—and even such basic equipment as a musket—to defend themselves, their families, and their forest farms. Indeed, when Conrad Weiser hurriedly organized a defensive force to repel Indian attacks in late October, hundreds of men turned out. Most produced adequate arms, "though about 20 had nothing but axes and pitchforks," Weiser wrote.

Many of the settlers who did own firearms lacked gunpowder and lead. When colonial leaders supplied them with ammunition, many lacked the courage to fight. "A great number are cowards," Weiser told Governor Morris.

Relatively few colonists had yet ventured into the valleys of what is now southern Schuylkill County. But when word spread of mid-October raids on settlements along the Susquehanna River, the hundred or so homesteaders north of the Blue Mountain between Port Clinton and Hamburg fled in terror. Those who hesitated found that Indian war parties swiftly searched them out and torched their farms.

"Our roads are continually full of travelers," wrote William Parsons, an Easton surveyor who had established a plantation about six miles south of the Blue Mountain, along the trail between Womelsdorf and Pine Grove. "Men, women and children, most of them barefoot, have been obliged to cross those terrible mountains with what little they could bring ... to get to the inhabitants on this side whilst those who live on this side near the mountain are removing their effects to Tulpehocken. Those at Tulpehocken are removing to Reading, and many at Reading are moving nigher to Philadelphia. ... For myself, I do not know whether I shall stay where I am, or leave all that I have to be destroyed by the barbarians."

Why had the Indians become violent? Conditions had clearly changed between 1681 and 1755, but what had happened to provoke the Indians? The first Europeans who immigrated to Penn's infant colony had struggled to establish themselves in the New World. The Native Americans they had encountered were peaceful and had generously provided the newcomers with land and food. How and why had the descendants of these friendly people developed into, in Parsons's word, barbarians?

The answers are complex. At first, the colonists congregated chiefly in southeastern Pennsylvania. The Europeans brought deadly new diseases, continually pressed the Native Americans for more land, and frequently treated individual Indians with disdain. Details of the Walking Purchase of 1737 in Bucks County show that even top-ranking officials in the Pennsylvania government weren't above cheating them.

In time, these and other factors combined to pressure Indians living along the Delaware into moving into the colony's interior. Within a few decades, the sons and daughters of Native Americans who had befriended William Penn on the lower Schuylkill River had resettled higher up in the Schuylkill watershed below the Blue Mountain. They lived chiefly in the Tulpehocken Valley, but only briefly. Even here, there was a steady influx of European colonists, and in 1732, head chief Sassoonan and lesser chieftains signed a paper in which they sold all rights to the Tulpehocken lands. These included "all those lands situate lying and being on the ... River Schuylkill and the branches thereof ..."

As payment, Pennsylvania authorities gave Sassoonan's band twenty gallons of rum and an assortment of trade goods that included mirrors, guns, hats, shoes, blankets, and ribbons. The colonials also made a monetary payment of fifty pounds.

During this time the Susquehanna Valley—which the Iroquois claimed by right of conquest of other tribes—was attracting many Indians who had been pushed from their traditional homelands. Many of Sassoonan's people moved to Shamokin, a growing Indian town at the confluence of the Susquehanna's North and West Branches. Indian cabins stood along the Susquehanna's east shore in present-day

Sunbury, on a large island in the North Branch, and on the point of land between the river's two branches within modern Northumberland.

At the same time, the Susquehanna was also beckoning to Indians who lived along the Chesapeake Bay and its tributary rivers. These included the Nanticokes.

In 1608 Captain John Smith, exploring from his base at Jamestown, Va., found these Indians living along the Nanticoke River on Maryland's eastern shore. Their women were farmers who raised corn, beans, squashes, and other vegetables. The men fished in the river and in the Chesapeake Bay and also hunted and trapped animals that lived on land. Their descendants later told missionaries who were studying Indian languages that in their own tongue, their name meant "the tidewater people."

As more and more Europeans settled in Maryland, the Nanticokes had many difficulties with their new neighbors, and at last they asked the Iroquois Confederacy for permission to relocate along the Susquehanna. The Iroquois allowed them to live on an island where the Juniata River flowed into the Susquehanna. An Iroquois spokesman explained to Pennsylvania officials this was necessary, because "the people of Maryland ... make slaves of them & sell their children for money."

In time, the Nanticokes moved higher up the Susquehanna and established a town on the North Branch at present Nanticoke in the Wyoming Valley. It appears that these Indians returned to their traditional homeland in Maryland with regularity.

Going to Maryland, they traveled down the Susquehanna in canoes and, when returning to the Wyoming Valley, took a shorter but much more mountainous overland trail through eastern Schuylkill County. This north-south path coursed from Calvert, Maryland, to Reading. It ran east of Lenhartsville before ascending the Blue Mountain and going through Tamaqua. Then the trail went through the gap

NANTICOKE PATH, NORTH

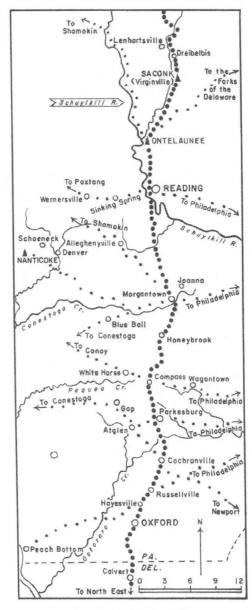

NANTICOKE PATH, SOUTH

(now used by Route 309) between Nesquehoning and Locust Mountains and headed north to Hazleton in Luzerne County and, eventually, Nanticoke.

South of the Blue Mountain, a secondary route split from the Nanticoke Path and, following the Schuylkill River, passed through the gap at Port Clinton. At some point above the mountain, this trail headed northwest toward the Indian town of Shamokin.

The Nanticoke Path and the spin-off route to Shamokin were part of a complex network of trails that Native Americans had blazed across Pennsylvania. By geographical coincidence, a trail known as the Tulpehocken Path linked the Indian settlement at Sunbury with the Tulpehocken Valley. Heading southeast from Sunbury, the route passed through the present Schuylkill County communities of Sacramento, Valley View, Hegins, Joliet, and through the gap at Ravine. South of Pine Grove, it went over the Blue Mountain and crossed the Tulpehocken Valley to its terminus at Womelsdorf, where it connected with an east-west trail to Philadelphia.

During William Penn's long peace, the Tulpehocken Path served as a major route for Iroquois diplomats and chiefs traveling to see the governor and other Pennsylvania colonial officials in Philadelphia. In turn, Pennsylvanians also used it when they traveled to the Iroquois territory in western New York. Early frontiersmen also called it the Shamokin Road.

But in 1755 war erupted in Pennsylvania. The previous year, French soldiers from Canada and colonial troops from Virginia had begun fighting for possession of the Ohio River Valley, where many Delaware Indians had settled after leaving central and eastern Pennsylvania. French officers encouraged Indians from many tribes to attack Pennsylvania and the other English colonies. Many Delaware warriors, angry that they had been forced from their traditional homelands, joined the French. Others fought because they wanted to stop the westward expansion of

Pennsylvania and other seaboard colonies.

Native Americans have left little information about their side of the conflict. That's a major reason why the telling of the story of the frontier war invariably becomes a lopsided accounting of atrocities committed by Indians against settlers and soldiers of European descent. Much of the historical record consists of journals, letters, and newspaper articles that were written by white frontiersmen who were more interested in shooting the Indians and collecting bounties on their scalps than in interviewing them and recording their version of the conflict. (Beginning in 1756, Pennsylvania paid bounties for the scalps of hostile Indians—$50 for those of females and $130 for the scalps of males over the age of ten.)

The historical record as written by white Pennsylvanians shows that the Shamokin path provided warriors on the Susquehanna with access to the frontier plantations. Although militia troops patrolled the base of the mountains, few ventured into the mountain valleys, and this gave war parties a measure of security as they followed the forest trail.

William Parsons, a skilled and frequent writer of letters, lived along the Tulpehocken Path below the mountains. When the French and Indian War broke out, he became a leader in defending the settlements. Parsons's accounts have preserved many details of the border war including the adventure of Adam Reed, who had established a farm in the forested valley near present Pine Grove.

One day in late October 1755, Reed "came to my house," Parsons wrote, "and declared that yesterday, between 11 and 12 o'clock, he heard three guns fired toward the plantation of his neighbor, Henry Hartman, which made him suspect that something more than ordinary had happened there. ... He took his gun and went over to Hartman's house, being about a quarter mile off, and found him lying dead upon his face. His head was scalped."

Reed scouted the woods around the Hartman

homestead, "but saw nobody else." Quickly but cautiously, the frontiersman hurried over the Blue Mountain to spread word south of the mountains about the killing.

Parsons promised Reed that he would come to Hartman's place to help with the burial, and the next morning he even set out for the desolate valley, "But when I got to the top of the mountain, I met some men who said they had seen two men lying dead and scalped in the Shamokin Road, about two or three miles from the place where we were," Parsons wrote.

Instead of riding on to Hartman's, "we altered our course, being 26 in number, and went to the place and found the two men, lying dead, about three hundred yards from each other, and all the skin scalped off their heads." The farmers had known the men, and someone remarked that one man, John Odwaller, had safely evacuated his family to the settlements south of Blue Mountain a few days earlier. Odwaller's homestead was at present-day Pine Grove, and he and his eleven-year-old daughter had returned to the farm "to fetch some of their effects that were left behind," Parsons wrote.

Father and daughter had encountered a war party as they reached the spot where the Tulpehocken Path forded the Swatara Creek just below its confluence with the Lower Swatara. When the rescuers arrived, Odwaller's daughter was missing, and "the other man had a wife and three or four children that are also missing," Parsons reported.

The farmers buried the dead men on the spot. "We got a grubbing hoe and spade, and dug a grave as best we could, the ground being very stony," Parsons said. "I thought it best to bury them to prevent their bodies from being torn to pieces by wild beasts."

With little ceremony, the settlers interred the farmers without removing their clothes or examining their wounds, although Parsons noted that in burying one man, "we saw that a bullet had gone through the leg."

Parsons and the others had little time for mourning. Even though they suspected that there were Indians still lurking about, they knew that they needed to organize a defense of the settlements and to salvage any foods or crops at homesteads hit by war parties.

"I can't help thinking," Parsons wrote, "that it would be well for a good number of the inhabitants to go next Monday and help to bring the poor people's grain and corn on this side of the mountain. It will help to maintain them, which we must do if they can't maintain themselves, and 'tis very likely those barbarous Indians will set fire to and burn all if it be not soon secured."

Settlers at Tulpehocken referred to a specific region as Allemengel, and this included the area around Snyders in southeastern Schuylkill County as well as the Berks County community of Albany. Allemengel was a particularly desolate place that was difficult to defend, and the few families living there decided to leave until the war ended. As the *Pennsylvania Gazette* reported in late March 1756, "10 wagons went up to Allemengel to bring down a family with their effects, and as they were returning ... were fired upon by a number of Indians from both sides of the road."

Terrified, the settlers jumped out of the wagons and "ran into the woods. ... The horses, frightened at the firing and terrible yelling of the Indians, ran down a hill and broke one of the wagons to pieces."

The warriors tracked down and killed five of the settlers, including a fourteen-year-old girl. "Another girl," the newspaper reported, "was shot in the neck and through the mouth and scalped." Despite these wounds, the girl survived and managed to escape.

By now, it was clear to everyone that the war parties had succeeded in making life quite dangerous for the few families occupying the valleys north of the Blue Mountain. Traveling east in June 1756, General James Young of the Pennsylvania Regiment rode along "an exceedingly bad road, very stony and mountainous" that led over the mountain near present Shartlesville. After that, "we passed by two plantations," the general wrote. "The rest of the country is chiefly barren."

At the Schuylkill River, Young came to Fort Lebanon and noted that it served as the refuge of some "country people ... in all six families." Riding farther east the same day, the general took a road that was little nothing more than "a narrow path, very hilly and swampy. ... Very few plantations on this road. Most of them deserted, and the houses burnt down."

Camp Followers Displease Army Chaplain

July 1756

Hostile Indians controlled the forests and mountains along the Susquehanna River during the summer of 1756. The French and Indian War was under way.

When Colonel William Clapham of the Pennsylvania Regiment's 3rd Battalion marched his regiment upriver from John Harris's trading post at present Harrisburg to build Fort Augusta at the confluence of the North and West Branches, he kept his troops ready for encounters with hostile forces. Accompanying the expedition was a flotilla of two canoes and twenty flat-bottom boats, manned by regimental boatmen and laden with provisions, supplies, cannons, and other big guns.

Clapham's column had stopped along the Susquehanna's east shore a short distance north of present-day Halifax and built a log fort to serve as a supply post for the much larger Fort Augusta.

The soldiers spent several weeks at the new fort, which Clapham named Fort Halifax, but on July 1 Clapham ordered them to head for the confluence.

Many of Clapham's soldiers had brought women on the expedition. These camp followers had many legitimate responsibilities, such as cooking, washing, mending clothing, and nursing ill or wounded troops.

Even so, their presence hardly pleased the regimental chaplain, the Rev. Charles Beatty.

As the regiment prepared to depart, the chaplain urged the colonel "to leave the women behind ..., especially those of bad character."

Although Fort Halifax occupied a lonely spot in the

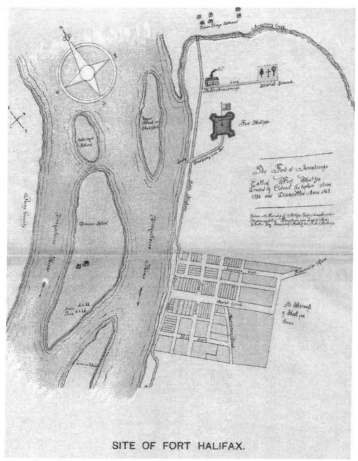

SITE OF FORT HALIFAX.

woods about twenty miles north of Harris's trading post, the clergyman was so persuasive that Clapham arranged for the women—there must have been at least a dozen—"to be paraded" for review and judgment, Beatty wrote in his journal.

As Clapham deliberated on the merits of the women, "one of the officers pleaded for one, and another for another, saying that they could wash, etc.," the chaplain noted.

In the end, few women were prohibited from tagging along, and, to Beatty's displeasure, even "these would not stay, but followed us that night and kept with us."

Entries in frontier diaries and official records indicate that women were often present at remote militia posts. In July 1756, for instance, a soldier deserted from Fort Shirley, a defense on Aughwick Creek south of present Mount Union. "Two Indian squaws ... went off with one of our men, a fellow that has formerly been an Indian trader," an officer noted in a military document.

In August 1756 drunken soldiers rioted at Fort Allen, which Benjamin Franklin had erected along the Lehigh River in the mountains north of modern Allentown. After attending a conference at Easton, some important Indians traveling to the Susquehanna River's North Branch had lodged overnight at the fort. During the evening, some of the soldiers spent the night with the Indian women.

According to Captain Reynolds's subsequent report, a number of inebriated soldiers became unruly, and the corporal of the guard got drunk, went berserk, and fired a gun "against a stone wall and broke her stock and tore the lieutenant's jacket."

Reynolds himself hadn't been at the fort that night, but learned later that a sergeant and five troops rode off for help even though the lieutenant forbade it. "They would not come back, the sergeant being drunk and as bad as the rest," Reynolds wrote.

As this suggests, discipline was frequently poor among soldiers on the Pennsylvania frontier. Many recruits had been farm hands or Indian traders prior to the war, which had started in 1755. Few had had any military experience, and many didn't respect their officers.

During his weeks at Fort Halifax, for example, Colonel Clapham had had to contend with a mutiny. Some soldiers were angry that they hadn't been paid and challenged their superiors. On June 20, the colonel reported he had twenty-six men in confinement.

War Party Springs Ambush near Plum Tree

August 1756

The story of Sunbury's "Bloody Spring" has been the subject of lore and legend for nearly 250 years.

Here are the facts, which, for all practical purposes, begin in July 1756 when soldiers in the Pennsylvania Regiment's 3rd Battalion marched to the forks of the Susquehanna River. By then, the Indian town called Shamokin, once the largest native settlement in Pennsylvania, had been burned and abandoned. Left over from the Indian settlement was a mature plum tree that a native gardener had cultivated.

The march upriver from modern Harrisburg took several weeks. Some troops came in boats or on horseback, but most walked.

The army, moving up the river's west shore, reached present-day Shamokin Dam on July 5, a Tuesday, and early that morning, Colonel William Clapham and Captain Joseph Shippen "went out in a boat and from the river saw five Indians in the fork, and, with a glass, saw others skulking on the hills."

But these Indians didn't interfere, and Clapham ordered his column to advance to the deserted town, which occupied the east bank. "We crossed over in bateaux, and I had the honor of being the first man to put his foot on shore at landing," Samuel Miles, one of the soldiers, recalled years afterward.

The Pennsylvanians took the high ground overlooking a large island in the North Branch without incident, and soon began the preliminary work needed to build Fort Augusta. A few men were assigned to tend the small herd of cows that Clapham had brought

Joseph Shippen

along as a source of milk and meat.

During the next three days, the colonel selected a site on the eastern riverbank a short distance back from the river. He decided to construct a fort in the shape of a great square with sides 204 feet long.

Work proceeded smoothly. In their quest for thick logs to serve as upright posts in the fort's walls, the soldiers began chopping down the forest that covered much of the floodplain. "Our fort is well built, being made from the largest logs we could find for a mile round," Captain Shippen soon reported.

The soldiers had a scare on Sunday, July 9, when, all at once, the cows started to bellow and run off. "It was supposed the Indians were driving them off," a soldier wrote.

Fearing an attack, the troops dropped their tools and ran for their guns. But no attack came, and in a while the soldiers went out to look for the cattle. Of twenty animals, they managed to locate only eleven, and nobody saw any Indians.

Bullock is an old fashioned word for a steer or ox, and in the 1750s, a soldier assigned to tend the cowherd was said to be a member of the bullock guard. Building the largest fortification on the Pennsylvania frontier took a lot of work, and the men must have consumed a good deal of fresh beef because military records show that a shipment of supplies sent upriver in late August—it actually arrived at Fort Augusta on September 1—included thirty-three cows.

Work progressed rapidly, and by mid-August, the walls were more than half completed. For the men who built it, the outpost became a relatively safe place. Not only were there several hundred soldiers, but the remote post also had considerable artillery—three cannons, two swivel guns, and two blunderbusses.

The colonel saw that his men took defensive measures during this time.

"Every morning before sunrise," Captain Shippen wrote on September 3, "a party of 50 men goes out to reconnoiter the ground for a mile and a half round the fort. They take different routes every time and march at the distance of six or seven yards apart, and all abreast in one rank ... so as to sweep a large space of ground."

A map reproduced in William Hunter's *Forts of the Pennsylvania Frontier* shows soldiers forming a long line that stretches along the river south of the fort. Commanded by a sergeant and corporals, and with soldiers spaced twenty-one feet apart, the line would extend well over one thousand feet. Using the fort as a hub, the column would cover a large semi-circle of ground, and in the process flush out any hostile Indians who might have crept into the area during the night.

But precautions such as this sometimes failed to scare off pro-French Indians at war with Pennsylvania and the other English colonies.

On August 23 Indians attacked two soldiers en route to Fort Augusta from a downriver post called Fort Halifax. They killed one soldier, but the other escaped and ran the few miles to Fort Augusta.

Six days later two men involved in building Fort Augusta, Samuel Miles and Samuel Atlee, took a walk across the floodplain on which the fort stood. They were hungry for fresh fruit, and "about half a mile from the fort stood a large tree that bore excellent plums in an open piece of ground ...," Miles wrote.

The tree was near a spring that flowed from the hillside east of the fort, and the officers walked over to the tree "to gather plums. While we were there, a party of Indians lay a short distance from us concealed in the thicket and had nearly gotten between us and the fort when a soldier belonging to a bullock guard ... came to the spring to drink. The Indians were thereby in danger of being discovered and ... fired at and killed the soldier," Miles said. "We ... returned to the fort in much less time than we were coming out."

Captain Shippen reported in a September 3 letter: "Last Sunday James Pattin, a soldier of my company, happened to go to a spring about a mile from the fort without arms (contrary to the orders given out), was shot by an Indian through the body and scalped and his skull split open in several places by a tomahawk."

The sound of gunshots triggered a quick reaction at Fort Augusta. "Two parties of 50 men each were immediately sent in pursuit of the enemy, but lost their tracks on the mountain," Shippen said. "They discovered the marks where two Indians had been sitting on the side of the hill in the bushes about 15 yards from the spring."

The Bloody Spring

Local legend holds that blood from Pattin's wounds ran into the spring and turned it red. The place where Pattin died has been known as Bloody Spring ever since.

But the soldier's death didn't slow work on the fort. On September 14 Peter Burd, the commissary officer, wrote, "the fort is now almost finished, and a fine one it is. We want a large flag to grace it."

Note: The state has erected a historical marker to call attention to the Bloody Spring, which is located about half a mile east of the site of Fort Augusta, where the Susquehanna River's floodplain meets the hill on Sunbury's east side.

Captive Farm Girl Finds Terror on the Trail

April 1758

In early April the nights can be cold, even frosty, in the mountains of Adams County in south-central Pennsylvania. The morning of April 5, Tom Jameson and his two oldest boys, Tom Jr. and John, dressed warmly before leaving the warmth of their log farmhouse to go outside and begin the day's chores. Inside, the other five members of the Jameson family were dressed appropriately for indoor activities.

"Mother was making preparations for breakfast," daughter Mary recalled years later.

Mary's mother, Jane Jameson, who had flowing red hair, had a family of eight to feed. Her children included two teenage girls, Betsy and Mary, and two younger boys, Matthew and Robert. There were also five guests that morning: a frontiersman named Robert Buck had brought his sister-in-law and her three children to stay with the Jamesons, if only temporarily. The woman's husband, William Mann, was a soldier in the Pennsylvania Regiment, stationed at Carlisle some forty miles to the north.

When the Indian war party attacked, Tom Jr. and John were inside the barn tending the cows and other livestock. Outdoors, their father stood alongside the log house, shaving a wooden handle to fit the hole in the head of an iron axe.

Buck, who had awakened early and ridden a horse to the Mann homestead, was returning to the Jameson farm when gunfire suddenly punctured the tranquil morning. Inside the cabin "everyone trembled with fear," Mary Jameson said later. Then they opened the door and saw that the "man and a horse lay dead near the house, having just been shot by the Indians." Six warriors emerged from the woods and ran toward the house. They were clad in leather leggings and breech clouts, their faces painted half red and half black.

They quickly captured Tom Jameson at the side of the house and rushed the house. Mrs. Jameson, Mrs. Mann, and the seven children didn't resist. The Indians made them all leave the cabin and go into the yard. As the warriors proceeded to plunder the house, four French soldiers in blue uniforms, who were part of the war party, came out of the woods. The Indians soon carried sacks of bread, smoked and dried meats, and dried meal from the cabin. They handed their booty to their captives. As the horrified prisoners watched, an Indian walked over to Buck's body and used a knife to cut the scalp from the top of his head.

Less than ten minutes after the attack began, the Indians hurriedly led the prisoners into the forest and headed west in a procession that went single file. The captives carried the loot from the cabin.

"On our march that day, an Indian went behind us with a whip, with which he frequently lashed the children to make them keep up," Mary Jameson said later.

The procession consisted of the six Indians, the four French soldiers, and ten captives: Tom and Jane Jameson, daughters Betsy and Mary, sons Matthew and Robert, and Mrs. Mann and her three children, one of whom was a little boy named John.

The Indians didn't know it, but during the commotion at the farmhouse, the two eldest Jameson boys had run from the barn and hidden in the forest.

Thus began the war party's eight-day trek across the Alleghenies to the Ohio country. The Jamesons and the Manns never did eat breakfast that day. As the Jamesons' daughter Mary, then a plucky girl of fifteen, years afterward described the ordeal:

"We traveled till dark, without a mouthful of food or a drop of water, although we had not eaten since the night before. Whenever the little children cried for

"The Taking of Mary Jemison" is historical artist Robert Griffing's masterful painting depicting that fateful day in April of 1758.

water, the Indians would make them drink urine, or go thirsty. At night they encamped in the woods, without fire and without shelter, where we were watched with the greatest vigilance. Extremely fatigued, and very hungry, we were compelled to lie upon the ground, supperless and without a drop of water to satisfy the cravings of our appetites."

The warriors roused their prisoners before first light the next morning, and resumed their march toward territory controlled by the French. "About sunrise we were halted, and the Indians gave us a full breakfast of provision that they had brought from my father's house," Mary Jameson recalled. Watchful for settlers or colonial soldiers who might attempt to rescue the captives, the war party hurried along a little-used path that led to the Allegheny Mountains.

The Indians took the captives into a thicket and fed them as evening came on. As darkness fell, an Indian took Mary and little John Mann away from their families and led them deeper into the bush, where they spent the night. When morning came, the other warriors and the French soldiers came up without the other prisoners.

Mary and John feared that the Indians had killed the others. Now wearing deerskin moccasins that one warrior had given them, the children did as told when the Indians ordered them to move out. The war party climbed a steep mountain, then descended into a valley and across a forest road used by Pennsylvania patrols traveling between two Pennsylvania posts, Fort Loudoun and Fort Littleton.

The warriors took pains to ensure that they left few tracks. As Mary subsequently reported, "They led us on as fast as we could travel, and one of them went behind and with a long staff picked up all the grass and weeds that we trailed down by going over them ... No one would have suspected that we had passed that way. ... After a hard day's march we encamped in a thicket, where the Indians made a shelter of boughs, and then built a good fire to warm and dry our benumbed limbs and clothing; for it had rained some through the day. Here we were again fed as before."

If Mary Jameson and John Mann had any doubts about the fate of their families, events at the campfire that evening made clear what had happened. To quote Mary,

When the Indians had finished their supper, they took from their baggage a number of scalps, and went about preparing them for the market, or to keep without spoiling, by straining them over small hoops which they prepared for that purpose, and then drying and scraping them by the fire. Having put the scalps, yet wet and bloody, upon the hoops, and stretched them to their full extent, they held them to the fire till they were partly dried, and then, with their knives, commenced scraping off the flesh; and in that way they continued to work, alternately drying and scraping them, till they were dry and clean. That being done, they combed the hair in the neatest manner, and then painted it and the edges of the scalps, yet on the hoops, red. Those scalps I knew at the time must have been taken from our family, by the color of the hair. My mother's hair was red; and I could easily distinguish my father's and the children's from each other. That sight was most appalling; yet I was obliged to endure it without complaining. In the course of the night, they made me to understand that they should not have killed the family, if the whites had not pursued them.

The war party continued its westward journey the next day, April 8, and that night "we encamped on the ground in the open air, without a shelter or fire," Mary said.

There was "continual falling of rain and snow" all day on April 9, the fifth day of her captivity. Even so, the Indians walked rapidly, and she and the boy ran in order to keep up. "At night the snow fell fast and the Indians built a shelter of boughs and a fire. ... Before the fire was kindled, I was ... much fatigued from running ..." As it happened, the fire and a hot supper revived her.

The late winter storm forced the war party to stay in this camp for several nights. On April 10 six other Indians came into the camp. They had also been raiding the Pennsylvania settlements, and they brought a prisoner—a young white man. Mary said that he looked "very tired and dejected. ... I was extremely glad to see him, though I knew from his appearance that his situation was as deplorable as mine, and that he could afford me no kind of assistance."

The arrival of the second war party meant there were now nineteen people at the mountain camp: twelve Indians, the four French soldiers, and the three prisoners.

The afternoon of April 11 one of the Indians shot a deer, which they dressed and then roasted whole. The animal provided what Mary called "a full meal" for the entire party, including the captives. "We were each allowed a share of their venison, and some bread, so that we had a good meal also," Mary said.

The weather cleared by April 12, and the travelers struck the trail early. They moved at a much slower pace, without an Indian walking in the rear to cover the tracks. In the afternoon, they came in sight of Fort Duquesne. Before they entered the post, they stopped and "the Indians combed the hair of the young man, the boy and myself, and then they painted our faces and hair red in the finest Indian style." They did this with considerable care,

The French Army had used logs and earthen fill to erect Fort Duquesne on a point of land at the confluence of the Allegheny and Monongahela Rivers. The fort's cannons commanded the Ohio River, which began at the confluence. The post was both a starting and returning point for war parties raiding Pennsylvania. On their way to the English settlements, warriors stopped at Fort Duquesne to receive arms and ammunition. On the return, they stopped to tell about their exploits and to receive rewards.

Mary Jameson and her fellow captives spent the night at the French post locked in a small log building inside the walls of the fort. In the morning, the French soldiers and Indians unlocked the door and took the boys. Mary never learned what happened to them. Later that morning Mary's captors ordered her out of the fort and into a canoe manned by two Seneca Indian women. The women pushed out and started down the Ohio, accompanied by a much larger canoe that carried the six warriors who had attacked the Jameson farm.

"When we set off," Mary said, "an Indian in the forward canoe took the scalps of my former friends, strung them on a pole that he placed upon his shoulder, and in that manner carried them, standing in the stern of the canoe directly before us, as we sailed down the river, to the town where the two squaws resided."

It took all day to reach the village of the Seneca women. It was night when the women landed their canoe on the river bank, but the men in the war canoe kept on going, and that "was the last I ever saw of them," Mary said.

The women adopted Mary to replace their brother, who had been killed, apparently the previous year, in fighting in Pennsylvania. They bathed her, helped her comb out her matted hair, and dressed her in new clothes—those of an Indian girl—to replace the tattered and soiled dress she had worn and slept in during her ordeal on the trail. They eventually taught her their language and their customs.

Mary lived as a Seneca Indian for the next seventy-five years. When she was eighty, she spent three days telling a New York State writer named James E. Seaver the story of her life. Although records in Pennsylvania list the spelling of Mary's family name as Jameson and Jamieson, Seaver spelled her surname as Jemison in her biography. This article is based on information that Seaver reported in his book, *A Narrative of the Life of Mrs. Mary Jemison*. Printed in 1824, it quickly became a bestseller.

Indian with Tomahawk Confronts Traveler

June 1763

A Quaker preacher, John Woolman, was in his early forties when he journeyed into the Pennsylvania frontier, headed for the Susquehanna River's North Branch.

It was June 1763, and as Woolman prepared to leave Philadelphia, "an express arrived from ... Pittsburgh, and brought news that the Indians had taken a fort ... and had slain and scalped English people."

Undaunted and with several Indians for guides, Woolman headed north toward the Wyoming Valley. He stopped one night at the Moravian community of Bethlehem, then traveled along the Lehigh River toward Fort Allen, a militia post that Ben Franklin had built seven years earlier at present-day Weissport.

Woolman learned that accommodations for frontier travelers were primitive. "We went forward on the ninth of the sixth month (June 9), and got lodging on the floor of a house, about five miles from Fort Allen," he wrote.

Along the way, "we met with an Indian trader lately come from Wyoming, and in conversation with him, I perceived that many white people do often sell rum to the Indians, which I believe is a great evil," Woolman wrote in his journal.

Woolman's party crossed the Lehigh near the fort on June 10. "The water being high, we went over in a canoe. Here we met an Indian, had friendly conversation with him, and gave him some biscuit; and he, having killed a deer, gave the Indians with us some of it," the traveler said.

John Woolman

Woolman and his guides pressed on. "After traveling some miles, we met several Indian men and women with a cow and horse, and some household goods, who were lately come from their dwelling at Wyoming, and were going to settle at another place. We made them some small presents. ...

"We pitched our tent near the banks of the same

73

river, having labored hard in crossing some of those mountains called the Blue Ridge," he wrote.

As he explored the campsite, Woolman was surprised to find paintings that Indian artists had made in the forest.

"Near our tent, on the sides of large trees peeled for that purpose, were various representations of men going to and returning from the wars, and of some being killed in battle. This being a path heretofore used by warriors, and ... I walked about viewing those Indian histories, which were painted mostly in red but some in black," he wrote.

It was the tenth of June—"Tenth of sixth month," according to the Quaker convention. "This was the first night that we lodged in the woods, and—being wet with traveling in the rain—the ground, our tent, and the bushes which we proposed to lay under our blankets, being also wet, all looked discouraging," Woolman wrote. "So we kindled a fire, with our tent open to it, and, with some bushes next the ground, and then our blankets, we made our bed, and, lying down, got some sleep. ... In the morning, feeling a little unwell, I went into the river; the water was cold, but soon after I felt fresh and well."

The travelers reached the Indian town at Wyoming, which is modern Wilkes-Barre, on June 13. They were distressed to learn than a runner had brought news that in western Pennsylvania Indian warriors had attacked an English fort near Pittsburgh.

Even worse, Indians at Wyoming told them that warriors had brought two scalps of white men, presumably from western Pennsylvania, to settlements along the North Branch "and told the people that it was war with the English."

That night, Woolman's guides arranged for the Quaker to lodge with an elderly man, and the traveler carried his baggage into the man's house. A while later, "I, perceiving there was a man near the door, went out," Woolman wrote.

The man "had a tomahawk wrapped under his

match-coat out of sight. As I approached him, he took it in his hand."

But the Quaker walked up to the Indian and addressed him in a friendly way. Woolman learned that the man spoke a little English, and, putting his weapon away, he then went "into the house with us, and, talking with our guides, soon appeared friendly, sat down and smoked his pipe."

The traveler noted in his journal that he had been startled to see the Indian suddenly brandish a hatchet. Nonetheless, "I believe he had no other intent than to be in readiness in case any violence was offered to him," Woolman wrote.

The next day, June 14, Woolman and his party visited with Indians living at Wyoming then continued their journey.

"We took our leave of them, we went up the river Susquehanna about three miles, to the house of an Indian called Jacob January." He had killed his hog, "and the women were making store of bread and preparing to move up the river. Here our pilots left their canoe when they came down in the spring, which, lying dry, was leaky." This detained the travelers for some hours, so that they "had a good deal of friendly conversation with the family; and, eating dinner with them, we made them some small presents. Then, putting our baggage in the canoe, some of them pushed slowly up the stream, and the rest of us rode our horses ... Swimming them over a creek called Lahawahamunk, we pitched our tent above it, there being a shower in the evening."

The Quaker's party continued, with the whites taking the trail along the river and the Indians canoeing up the North Branch.

"We proceeded forward till the afternoon, when, a storm appearing, we met our canoe at an appointed place and, the rain continuing, we stayed all night." The rainfall was "so heavy that it beat through our tent and wet us and our baggage." The next day "we found ... abundance of trees blown down by the storm ... and had occasion reverently to consider the kind dealings of the Lord who provided a safe place for us in a valley while this storm continued." The large number of downed trees hindered their progress, "and in some swamps our way was so stopped that we got through with extreme difficulty."

Despite the weather, the travelers encountered an Indian bound for Fort Augusta, some sixty miles downriver.

"This afternoon Job Chilaway, an Indian from Wyalusing, who talks good English and is acquainted with several people in and about Philadelphia, met our people on the river," Woolman wrote. "Understanding where we expected to lodge, he pushed back about six miles, and came to us after night; and in a while our own canoe came, it being hard work pushing up the stream. Job told us that an Indian came in haste to their town yesterday and told them that three warriors, coming from some distance, lodged in a town above Wyalusing a few nights past, and that these three men were going against the English at Juniata. Job was going down the river to the province-store at Shamokin (present-day Sunbury)."

On June 17, "we ... reached Wyalusing about the middle of the afternoon," Woolman wrote. "After a while we heard a conch-shell blow several times, and then came John Curtis and another Indian man, who kindly invited us into a house near the town, where we found, I suppose, about sixty people sitting in silence."

Woolman reported that he spent several days in the village, where a Moravian missionary had come to preach. He visited with the Indians and found the Moravian missionary to be friendly. The Quaker left on June 21, headed downriver.

Before he departed, Woolman sketched this description of Wyalusing:

This town stands on the bank of the Susquehanna, and consists, I believe, of about forty houses, mostly compact together, some about thirty feet long and eighteen wide, some bigger, some less; mostly built of split plank, one end set in the ground, and the other pinned to a plate on which lay rafters, and are covered with bark. I understand a great flood last winter overflowed the chief part of the ground where the town stands, and some were now about moving their houses to higher ground.

We expected only two Indians to be of our company, but when we were ready to go, we found many of them were going to Bethlehem with skins and furs, who chose to go in company with us. So they loaded two canoes in which they desired us to go, telling us that the waters were so raised with the rains that the horses should be taken by such as were better acquainted with the fording-places. So we, with several Indians, went in the canoes, and others went on horses, there being seven besides ours.

They met with the horsemen once on the way by appointment, and that night they camped a little below a branch called Tankhannah. "Some of the young men, going out a little before dusk with their guns, brought in a deer."

In time, they left the Susquehanna River and headed south, eventually coming to the upper reaches of the Lehigh River.

By June 24, the travelers had reached Fort Allen on the Lehigh. They had "forded the westerly branch of the Delaware (the Lehigh) three times." This, Woolman said, was shorter than going over the top of the mountains called the Second Ridge. "In the second time (of) fording where the river cuts through the mountain, the waters being rapid and pretty deep, and my companion's mare, being a tall, tractable animal, he sundry times drove her back through the river, and they loaded her with the burthens of some small horses which they thought not sufficient to come through with their loads."

Woolman returned to his home near Philadelphia within a few days and, reflecting on his trip, wrote this summary: "Between the English settlements and Wyalusing we had only a narrow path, which in many

77

places is much grown up with bushes, and interrupted by abundance of trees lying across it. These, together with the mountains, swamps and rough stones, make it a difficult road to travel, and the more so for ... rattlesnakes abound here, of which we killed four."

Even Indians Get Lost, Hungry in the Forest

Spring 1773

Witchcraft was common among Native American tribes in Pennsylvania, and many people who lived on the American frontier had a genuine fear of being bewitched. But they also harbored deep fears of getting lost in the forest and then starving to death or being killed by wild beasts.

Many who met untimely deaths were European colonists who came to the woods with few survival skills, but others were Indians who had spent their entire lives in the forest.

In 1773, for instance, a party of twenty Indians was traveling through Ohio, accompanied by John Heckewelder, a Moravian missionary. These Indians had moved to the Ohio country from Wyalusing on the Susquehanna River's North Branch the previous year. Only the Indian serving as their guide was familiar with the countryside.

It was springtime, and severe flooding along major streams had delayed their journey. Soon their provisions ran out, and one morning every man who had a rifle went out looking for game. The hunters included Papunhank, a Delaware Indian who had been prominent in Pennsylvania some years earlier. Most hunters came back empty-handed, but not Papunhank. He got lost in the woods and didn't come back at all.

Another man, the travelers' guide, managed to shoot a wild cat, which the Indians cooked but declined to eat. Even though they were extremely hungry, they didn't consider the flesh of a wild cat as suitable for human consumption.

THE GREAT SHAMOKIN TI
- WESTERN PART -

The guide went out again the next morning, this time looking for Papunhank as well as for game. He walked five or six miles before he found the lost Indian "with a fine deer that he had killed," Heckewelder wrote. "The sight of these two men dragging along a large deer was truly joyful to us." Not only was Papunhank rescued, but there was also meat for everyone.

Not all travelers were so fortunate. Heckewelder, who spoke several Indian languages and recorded many details of Native American life, also wrote about an Indian family's gruesome encounter with hardship, hunger, and horror on the trail.

The Great Shamokin Path, an ancient route, connected native settlements high up on the Susquehanna's West Branch with Indian towns on the Allegheny River. Indian people would take this route when traveling from region to region. The trail ran

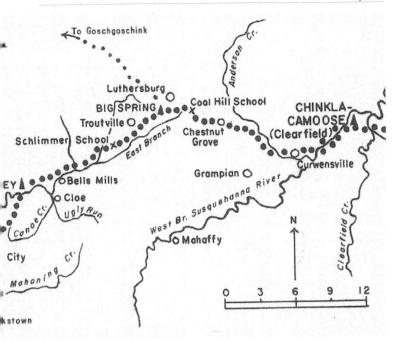

from Kittanning on the Allegheny, crossed Big Island (across from present-day Lock Haven), and stretched east to the Forks of the Susquehanna where it reached Shamokin, a major Indian town during the 1700s.

As winter approached in 1739, an Indian woman who lived west of the Allegheny wanted to visit relatives or friends. She decided that she and her three children would walk across the mountains to the Delaware Indian town at Big Island.

She failed to anticipate that winter would set in early and would bring much snow. She and the children had reached the West Branch, but were still far west of Big Island when she realized they couldn't go on.

"She began with putting herself and her children on short allowances (of food) in hopes that the weather might become more moderate or the snow so hard that they could walk over it," Heckewelder said.

81

"She strove to make her little store of provisions last as long as she could by using the grass which grew on the river's edge," he wrote. The woman also boiled the bark from certain types of trees in order to make them digestible.

But the snow kept falling, and soon it was six feet deep. She found as much wood as she could and built a campfire. If its flames kept her and the children from freezing to death, it also served as a weapon. There were "wolves hovering about night and day, often attempting to rush into her little encampment," Heckewelder said. When they approached, she repelled them "by throwing out firebrands to them."

The day came when all their food was gone, and "her situation at last became intolerable," Heckewelder said.

Desperate, she decided to kill her youngest child and feed its flesh to its siblings "in order to preserve the others and herself from the most dreadful death," Heckewelder wrote. She thought she could stave off starvation until the weather broke. But the wolves were also starving, and, "getting the scent of the slaughtered child, became more furious than ever before ..."

The woman prayed to the Great Spirit for rescue, "but still the danger increased, the horrid food was almost exhausted, and no relief came," Heckewelder said.

Knife in her hand, she was preparing to sacrifice a second child when suddenly she heard "the yell of two approaching Indians." They had traveled over the snow on snowshoes, and brought enough provisions to feed the surviving children and the mother.

The missionary reported that a premonition or a dream had prompted the rescuers to venture out on the trail in search of someone who had become lost.

The men made snowshoes "for the woman to walk on, and brought her and her children along in safety to Big Island, where my informants resided at the time," Heckewelder said.

John Heckewelder

The missionary added, "The place where this awful event took place was since called Enda Mohatink, which means 'where human flesh was eaten.'"

If the natural elements posed danger to Native Americans, they were also vulnerable to what they regarded as supernatural forces. Heckewelder's accounts of Indian life in Pennsylvania, Ohio, and other regions make it clear that many of the native people he knew believed the sorcerers could cast fatal spells on them. If bewitched, they would waste away and die.

Heckewelder's 1818 book, *History, Manners and Customs of the Indians Nations Who Once Inhabited Pennsylvania and the Neighboring States* contains one of the strangest anecdotes in frontier literature: In

1776, a Quaker named John Anderson challenged two Indian sorcerers "to try their art on his person and do him all the harm that they could by magical means." Anderson wanted one sorcerer to cast his spells on one day, and the second on the next day.

Fearing for Anderson's safety, Indian leaders objected to the test, but summoned two leading sorcerers when he persisted. The first refused to participate. He told Anderson that he only used his magical powers against bad people and that "Anderson was so good and so honest a man ... and the friend of all Indians that he could not think of doing him an injury."

The second sorcerer had no such reservations and, with many spectators present, attempted to bewitch the Quaker. He sat on the ground about twelve feet from where Anderson was sitting and did his best to enchant him. But after several hours, he conceded that he had failed and explained that salt protected people against his magical powers, and that Anderson and other white people used much salt on their food.

Heckewelder also reported an encounter with an Indian rain-maker, who during a severe drought in 1799 predicted—and then claimed credit for—the rain that fell for several hours on an otherwise clear day. "All at once the horizon became overcast and without any thunder or wind it began to rain," Heckewelder wrote. The missionary preferred to believe the man was an astute observer of natural phenomena who had correctly interpreted natural phenomena rather than the possessor of any special powers over the weather.

'Howdy,' Warrior Says to Startled Farmer

June 1778

A Wyoming Valley settler, Luke Swetland turned forty-nine the summer of 1778.

"I lived at Wyoming on the Susquehanna River at the time when it was cut off by the Indians, and with my family was captivated with many others, on condition of being subject to the king and had liberty to live on our farms, the articles of capitulation were made and signed July 5, 1778," Swetland wrote.

That must have been galling. After all, Swetland had enlisted in the Continental Army in 1776 and served under General George Washington. His company camped at Valley Forge during the hard winter of 1777-78.

When Washington learned the British intended to raid the Susquehanna Valley in '78, he allowed Swetland and other troops to return to their frontier homes to help protect the western settlements.

The Indians and British invaded the North Branch in early summer, and the Wyoming settlers rallied to repel them. The defeat they suffered was called the Wyoming Massacre. Swetland himself didn't fight. Instead, he had been stationed at a stockade post called Forty Fort near Wilkes-Barre during the battle.

Terms of the surrender prohibited the Indians and the British from destroying the North Branch settlements, "but they soon broke the agreement by burning buildings, killing and driving off our cattle, sheep, horses and hogs, and plundering everything they could find," Swetland reported.

At last the invaders withdrew upriver to southern New York, and the Swetlands returned to their farm.

"We found some of our cattle ... one ox, one milch (milk) cow, and four young cattle, so (we) concluded we would try to live there ... and so picked up the small matter the Indians had left us, and went to keeping house," Swetland said.

The Swetland family had come to Wyoming in 1769. They were among the Connecticut settlers who had moved into northeastern Pennsylvania believing their colony had purchased the valley from the Iroquois. After all these years on the North Branch, they weren't willing to abandon their homestead.

"We took courage and went to work at harvesting and haying, but about 10 days after ... two or three Indians came and told us that the Indians were returning with some wild Indians that had not been with them in the battle nor plundering, and if we were not all gone in the space of two hours, we should all be scalped."

The Swetlands left quickly.

"Having no horses ... I and my wife and four sons, the oldest of them about 14 years old, set out on foot, took as much victuals as we could well carry and a few trifles out of the house, and went to Delaware River to Colonel Strouds, where we were supported some days on the public continental stores until a party of continental soldiers, together with a number of the Susquehanna inhabitants, were going back to retake the place."

No stranger to strife, "I went with them to harvest my English grain," Swetland said.

He reaped a quantity of wheat, and on August 24, he and a friend, Joseph Blanchard, "went down the Susquehanna River in a canoe about eight miles below Wilksbury fort" to a grist mill that some settlers had built on a creek near present Nanticoke.

"Having carried our wheat to the mill and got it floured, I borrowed the miller's horse to carry my flour to the canoe. Blanchard had his flour on his back," Swetland said.

They failed to see six Indians who had "hid under

the weeds and bushes close by the path."

The Indians emerged suddenly and grabbed the unsuspecting Blanchard and Swetland. "Howdy!" a warrior said.

The settlers were so startled, they offered no resistance. The Indians tied them together and led them quickly upriver as prisoners of war.

Swetland and Blanchard survived their first day as Indian captives partly by eating berries they picked along the trail.

As Swetland reported later, the war party that had captured them consisted of "six savages naked and dismally painted in red and black." The Indians had tied them together with a rope, and, forcing them to take off their shoes, gave them moccasins to wear on the trek north to the Iroquois country in western New York.

The Indians made them change footwear because the softer soles of the moccasins left less of an imprint on the forest floor than did European-style shoes and boots. Any soldiers who tried to catch the war party would have a harder time in tracking the moccasin-clad travelers. "We went about 10 miles that night and made a halt, struck up a fire, and they laid us on our backs, pinioned (tied) our arms behind us, tied round the neck and middle. ... One of the Indians lay on the rope between us," Swetland said.

Swetland's phrase "struck up a fire" suggests that the fire maker literally struck a piece of iron against a chunk of flint so that sparks fell onto flammable material such as the bark from certain trees that the Indians carried with them.

Swetland didn't report that the warriors cooked or ate anything that first night. He said that the war party went thirty hours without eating, and that he and Blanchard ate berries that they found growing on bushes along the trail.

On the second day, "some time after noon, they made a stop and ate some roasted hog's flesh, and gave some to me and my fellow prisoner."

To be sure, Swetland, as a soldier in Washington's army in 1776 and 1777, wasn't a stranger to physical hardships. But he found conditions along the trail quite harsh. As it turned out, Swetland survived the ordeal and eventually wrote a book entitled *A Very Remarkable Narrative of Luke Swetland.*

Swetland hardly painted a flattering portrait of the warrior who had captured him.

"The Indian that first took hold of me said he was my master and drove me before him ... and would often strike me with his tomahawk on my hips and sides," he said.

These blows evidently weren't struck by the tomahawk's cutting edge, but they quickly caused bruises.

Also, Swetland said that after hitting him, the Indian frequently exclaimed, "tullaway" and "God damn tullaway." The frontiersman didn't record what "tullaway" meant.

To his discomfort, Swetland discovered that the soles of the moccasins were much softer than the soles of his shoes. He said that his feet soon became sore "for they made me throw away my shoes and gave me deerskin moccasins, and being forced to run where the ground was stony made ... bruises on the bottoms of my feet."

The prisoner also came to dread the war party's occasional rest stops.

The warrior who had custody of Swetland carried a flintlock musket or rifle called a firelock. To prime the gun for firing, he put gunpowder into a special receptacle called a pan. This powder was often referred to as "priming powder," but Swetland just called it "priming."

"My master ... would often call to me and say, 'come in, my dog,' as much as to say, 'come here, my dog.'"

Swetland added that when he obediently walked over to the Indian, the man "would cock his firelock, and put it to my breast and grin and put his finger to the trigger with an air of much fury. At first I thought it was the last moment of my life, but I said and did nothing.

"He seeing I paid no regard to that, took it from my breast, opened the pan and threw out the priming and primed it anew and then put it to my forehead with the same furious motions as before," Swetland wrote.

But the warrior didn't shoot him that time either.

As it turned out, the frontiersman survived a captivity of about thirteen months. In 1785, he published the sixteen-page narrative on which this article is based.

Gunfire Startles Women Milking Cows

June 1778

The Rev. Philip Vickers Fithian, a Presbyterian missionary, kept a detailed journal as he traveled through the Susquehanna River Valley in 1775.

For a preacher on the move, he spent considerable time visiting "the two infant villages" of Sunbury and Northumberland.

His daily entries captured the spirit of the era.

On June 28, for instance, there was excitement in Northumberland when "about 12 o'clock marched into this town from the Great Island ... 50 miles up the river (West Branch) 30 young fellows, all expert riflemen, with a drum and a fife, under Captain Lowdon." The frontiersmen were headed for Massachusetts, where fighting had occurred at Lexington, Concord, and Boston.

A few days later, a post rider delivered some newspapers from Philadelphia. They contained "accounts of the battle of Bunker Hill" and reported that Gen. George Washington was just "leaving Philadelphia for the North American camp."

If war had disrupted life in distant New England, the Susquehanna Valley was tranquil. People were concerned about political and military events in Massachusetts and elsewhere, but day-to-day events on the farm and in town tended to keep them occupied with domestic matters.

As Fithian traveled, he found valley farmers cultivating oats, wheat and rye. They didn't always build fences around their pastures. Instead, they put bells on their livestock, then turned them loose to forage in the woods nearby. In the early evening, the

Charcoal drawing of Philip Vickers Fithian, Class of 1772, by an unknown artist., ca. October 1776.

bells served as a guide for farm children sent out "to find and bring in the cows."

As a result, "the woods are musical; they are harmonious," Fithian noted. "Bells tinkling from every quarter make a continued and cheering echo. Cows returning home. Sheep and horses grazing through the

91

woods, and those all around in every part make a transporting vesper."

The missionary also reported a continuing influx of new settlers to the region. "Rapid, most rapid, is the growth of this country," Fithian noted in his July 18 entry, written at Northumberland. "Two wagons, with goods, cattle, women, tools, etcetera went through the town today from East Jersey, on their way to Fishing Creek up the river, where they are to settle."

This tranquility didn't last. As the war progressed, pro-British Indians terrorized the valley, and the commandant at Fort Augusta, which Fithian had visited while staying at Sunbury, found himself responsible for protecting the region.

In one instance, in early 1778, Col. Samuel Hunter organized a militia company of about twenty men to defend the Fishing Creek settlements near present-day Bloomsburg. The lieutenant was a twenty-one-year-old scout named Moses Van Campen, who had been born in Hunterdon County, N,J,, and had grown up on his father's farm in the North Branch Valley.

Van Campen soon built a fort on Fishing Creek by erecting a log stockade around the house of a farmer named Wheeler. The farmhouse stood on high ground overlooking the creek, about three miles above the North Branch.

The stockade was large enough to accommodate all the farm families in the neighborhood. For most of 1778, they stayed inside the fort at night and worked on their farms during the day—provided, of course, the militia patrols said the woods were safe.

Towards evening, the farmers would drive their cows back to Fort Wheeler, where Van Campen had constructed a fenced-in cattle yard on the flood plain a short distance below the fort. After the farmers secured the cows in the pen, the women brought pails and stools down to the enclosure. They placed the pails under the cows, then sat on the stools to do the milking.

As Van Campen years later told his grandson and

biographer, John N. Hubbard:

On one evening in the month of June, just at the time when the women and the girls were milking their cows, a sentinel called my attention to a movement in some bushes not far off ... Indians (were) making their way to the cattle yard.

There was no time to be lost. I immediately selected ten of my sharp shooters and under cover of a rise of ground, crept between them and the milkers. On ascending the ridge, we found ourselves within pistol shot of our lurking foes.

I fired first and killed the leader. This produced an instant panic among the (war) party, and they all flew away like a flock of birds. A volley from my men did no further execution. It only made the woods echo with the tremendous roar of their rifles.

But the sudden sound of gunfire also terrified the women and the cows. The women were "terribly frightened ... they started up upon their feet, screamed aloud, and ran with all their might ... the milk pails flew in every direction, and the milk was scattered to the winds.

"The best runner got in (to the fort) first. The poor cattle, equally frightened, leapt the fence and ran off into the woods in every direction with their tails up, and bellowing at a most terrible rate.

"It was a scene of confusion as wild, and to us who knew there was no danger, as laughable as can be well imagined. But ... to the timid women and girls it was a serious fright, for when we returned we found them trembling with agitation and their faces pale from fear."

Selected Bibliography

Brainerd, David. *Memoirs of Rev. David Brainerd, Missionary to the Indians of North America.* Edited by J. M. Sherwood. New York and London: Funk & Wagnalls Company, 1884.

Franklin, Benjamin. *The Autobiography of Benjamin Franklin.* New York, Walter J. Black, 1932.

Heckewelder, John Gottlieb Ernestus. *A Narrative of the Mission of the United Brethren among the Delaware and Mohegan Indians: from its Commencement, in the Year 1740, to the Close of the Year 1808; Comprising All the Remarkable Incidents Which Took Place at Their Missionary Stations During That Period; Interspersed With Anecdotes, Historical Facts, Speeches of Indians, and Other Interesting Matters.* Philadelphia: McCarty & Davis, 1820.

Heckewelder, John. *History, Manners, and Customs of the Indian Nations, Who Once Inhabited Pennsylvania and the Neighboring States.* Philadelphia: Publication Fund of the Historical Society of Pennsylvania, 1876. (Reprinted by Arno Press Inc., 1971.)

Hubbard, John N. *Sketches of the Life and Adventures of Moses Van Campen, A Surviving Officer of the Army of the Revolution.* Dansville, N.Y.: George W. Stevens, 1841. (Reprinted by Garland Publishing Inc., New York, 1977.)

Levering, Bishop J. Mortimer. *An Account of the Massacre at Gnadenhuetten, Pa.* Vol. VII, Transactions of the Moravian Historical Society. Nazareth, Pa.: Printed for the Society, 1906.

Loskiel, George Henry. *History of the Mission of the*

United Brethren among the Indians in North America. London: printed for The Brethren's Society for the Furtherance of the Gospel; 1794.

Seaver, James. *A Narrative of the Life of Mrs. Mary Jemison.* Canandaigua, N. Y.: J. D. Beamis and Co., 1824. (Reprinted by Garland Publishing Inc., New York, 1977.)

Swetland, Luke. *A Very Remarkable Narrative of Luke Swetland.* Hartford, 1785. (Reprinted by Garland Publishing Inc., New York, 1977.)

Swift, Robert B. *The Mid-Appalachian Frontier: A Guide to Historic Sites of the French and Indian War.* Gettysburg, Pa.: Thomas Publications, 2001

Hubbard, John N. *Sketches of the Life and Adventures of Moses Van Campen, A Surviving Officer of the Army of the Revolution.* Dansville, N.Y.: George W. Stevens, 1841. (Reprinted by Garland Publishing Inc., New York, 1977.)

Wallace, Paul A. W. *Conrad Weiser, 1696-1760, Friend of Colonist and Mohawk.* Philadelphia, University of Pennsylvania Press, 1945.

Wallace, Paul A.W. *Indian Paths of Pennsylvania.* Harrisburg: Pennsylvania Historical and Museum Commission, 1993.

Woolman, John. *The Journal, With Other Writings of John Woolman.*Edited by Ernest Rhys. London: J. M. Dent & Sons, Ltd.; New York, E. P. Dutton & Co., 1910.

45824252R00063

Made in the USA
Charleston, SC
28 August 2015